NEW
RHYMING
DICTIONARY
OF
ONE AND TWO
SYLLABLE
RHYMES

||||| **BARNES & NOBLE BOOKS**
DIVISION OF HARPER & ROW, PUBLISHERS
New York, Hagerstown, San Francisco, London

Distributed in
the U.S. by
Harper & Row, Publishers, Inc.,
10 East 53rd St.
New York, N.Y. 10022

CONTENTS

)

PRONUNCIATION GUIDE

a *as in* at	o *as in* rod
ā *as in* gāte	ō *as in* ōld
ȧ *as in* ȧkin	ö *as in* wön
â *as in* fâre	ô *as in* fôr
ä *as in* cär	oi *as in* oil
ă *as in* ăll	oo *as in* good
ay *as in* bay	ōō *as in* tōō
	ou *as in* out
e *as in* end	ow *as in* owl
ē *as in* hē	oy *as in* boy
ė *as in* dėfy	
ê *as in* hêr	
ēe *as in* sēen	u *as in* pup
ew *as in* new	ū *as in* ūnit
	û *as in* ûrn
i *as in* ill	
ī *as in* īce	
î *as in* sîr	y *as in* try
	ẏ *as in* mẏth

PREFACE

This rhyming dictionary is a valuable reference book for both experienced and amateur writers of rhyme and verse. Besides normal rhyming words, geographical names, proper nouns, scientific terms and slang words have been included to make this book more complete.

It is divided into two parts—one syllable and two or more syllable rhyme endings. The one syllable endings are those of one or more syllables that rhyme on the last syllable only. For example: -āke: ache, bake; betake, etc. The two syllable endings are those of two syllables or more that rhyme on the last two or more syllables. For example: -āker: acre, baker, faker, etc. All rhyme endings are listed alphabetically in both sections.

In creating rhymes, poetic license is often used. Poetic license includes forced rhymes such as -iddle and -ittle, -aft and -affed; the use of contractions such as -in' (-ing) to rhyme with -in and -en; and accenting normally unaccented syllables such as hurricane and porcelain. Throughout the dictionary there are abundant cross references to help in these areas.

As an added aid, a useful glossary of poetic terms can be found in the back of this dictionary.

THE EDITORS.

ONE SYLLABLE RHYMES

-ä, -äh: ah, baa, bah, blah, bra, fa, ha, la, ma, pa, shah, spa; faux pas, hurrah, mama, papa; algebra, cha cha cha, cinema, fistula. (And many other false rhymes ending in "à" such as "America".)

-ab: bab, blab, cab, crab, dab, drab, gab, grab, jab, Mab, nab, scab, slab, stab, tab; bedab, confab, Punjab; taxicab. (For rhymes to "swab," see -ob.)

-äbe: Abe, babe, wabe; outgrabe (Lewis Carroll); astrolabe.

-ac, -ack: bac, back, black, cack, clack, claque, crack, hack, jack, Jack, knack, lac, lack, "mack", Mac, pack, plaque, quack, rack, sac, sack, sacque, shack, slack, smack, snack, stack, tack, thwack, track, whack, wrack, yak; aback, alack, attack, bivouac, bootblack, cognac, drawback, gimcrack, haystack, horseback, knapsack, ransack, shellac; almanac, Appotomac, bric-a-brac, cardiac, haversack, maniac, Sarawak, stickleback, zodiac; demoniac; hypochondriac, sacroiliac.

-äce, -äse: ace, base, bass, brace, case, chase, dace, face, grace, Grace, lace, mace, pace, place, plaice, race, space, Thrace, trace, vase; abase, apace, bullace, debase, deface,

1

disgrace, displace, efface, embrace, encase, grimace, horse-race, misplace, outface, replace, retrace, staircase, transplace, uncase, unlace; commonplace, interlace, interspace, market-place, populace, steeplechase.

-ach, -atch: batch, catch, hatch, latch, match, patch, ratch, scratch, slatch, snatch, thatch; attach, detach, dispatch, unlatch; unattach. (For rhymes to "watch", see -otch.)

-act: act, bract, fact, pact, tact, tract; abstract, attract, co-act, compact, contact, contract, detract, distract, enact, epact, exact, extract, impact, infract, intact, protract, react, redact, refract, retract, subtract, transact; cataract, counteract, overact, re-enact, retroact; matter-of-fact. (Extend -ack for "blacked" and other preterites.)

-ad: ad, add, bad, brad, cad, chad, clad, dad, fad, gad, glad, had, lad, mad, pad, plaid, sad, scad, shad, tad; Bagdad, bedad, begad, footpad, monad, nomad; ironclad, olympiad, Stalingrad. (For rhymes to "wad," see -od.)

-āde, -āid: aid, bade, blade, braid, cade, fade, glade, grade, jade, lade, laid, maid, neighed, paid, plaid, raid, shade, skaid, Slade, sleighed, spade, stade, staid, suède, they'd, trade, wade, weighed; abrade, afraid, arcade, Belgrade, blockade, brigade, brocade, cascade, charade, cockade, crusade,

2

decade, degrade, dissuade, evade, grenade, home-made, housemaid, invade, limeade, mermaid, nightshade, okayed, orangeade, parade, persuade, pervade, prepaid, stockade, unlade, unlaid, unmade, unpaid, upbraid, waylaid; accolade, ambuscade, balustrade, barricade, cannonade, cavalcade, citigrade, colonnade, custom-made, enfilade, escalade, esplanade, gasconade, lemonade, marmalade, masquerade, orangeade, overlade, overlaid, palisade, pasquinade, plantigrade, promenade, renegade, retrograde, serenade, underlaid, underpaid. (Also see "flayed", "grayed", and many other preterites of verbs ending in **-ay** and **-ey**.)

-āfe: chafe, Rafe, safe, strafe, waif; unsafe.

-adge: badge, cadge, fadge, Madge.

-adze: adze. (See plurals of words in **-ad**.)

-aff: calf, chaff, gaff, graph, half, quaff, staff, Taff; behalf, carafe, distaff, giraffe, Llandaff, riff-raff, seraph; autograph, cenotaph, epitaph, paragraph, phonograph, photograph, telegraph; cinematograph.

-aft: aft, chaffed, craft, daft, draft, draught, graft, haft, Kraft, laughed, quaffed, raft, shaft, staffed, "straffed", Taft, waft; abaft, aircraft; handicraft. (Also preterites of **-aff** words.)

3

-ag: bag, brag, crag, dag, drag, fag, flag, gag, hag, jag, knag, lag, nag, quag, rag, sag, scrag, shag, slag, snag, stag, swag, tag, wag; dishrag, grabbag, sandbag, zigzag.

-āge: age, cage, Drage, gage, gauge, page, rage, sage, stage, swage, wage; assuage, engage, enrage, greengage, outrage, presage; disengage, overage. (And nearly 100 false rhymes in words ending in -age in which the final syllable is not accentuated, such as "sausage", "advantage".)

-åge: see -idge.

-ague: Hague, plague, Prague, vague.

-āid: See -āde.

-āil, -āle: ail, ale, bail, bale, brail, Braille, dale, fail, flail, frail, gale, Gail, Grail, hail, hale, jail, kail, kale, mail, male, nail, pail, pale, quail, rail, sail, sale, scale, shale, snail, stale, swale, tail, tale, they'll, trail, vale, veil, wale, whale, wail, Yale; assail, avail, bewail, blackmail, bobtail, cocktail, curtail, detail, dovetail, entail, exhale, female, hobnail, impale, inhale, prevail, regale, retail, travail, unveil, wagtail, wassail, wholesale; Abigail, countervail, farthingale, nightingale.

-āim, -āme: aim, blame, came, claim, dame, fame, flame, frame, game, lame, maim,

4

name, same, shame, tame; acclaim, aflame, became, declaim, defame, disclaim, exclaim, inflame, misname, nickname, proclaim, reclaim, surname ; overcame.

-āin, -āne: ain (Scotch), bane, blain, brain, Cain, cane, chain, crane, Dane, deign, drain, fain, fane, feign, gain, grain, Jane, lain, lane, main, Maine, mane, pain, pane, plain, plane, rain, reign, sane, Seine, skein, slain, Spain, sprain, stain, strain, swain, thane, thegn, train, twain, vain. vane, vein, wain, wane, zane; abstain, again, airplane, amain, arraign, attain, biplane, campaign, Champagne, chicane, chilblain, chow mein, cocaine, complain, constrain, contain, detain, disdain, distrain, domain, Duquesne, Elaine, enchain, engrain, entrain, explain, germane, henbane, humane, inane, insane, Louvain, maintain, membrane, misfeign, moraine, murrain, obtain, ordain, pearmain, pertain, plantain, profane, ptomaine, refrain, regain, remain, restrain, retain, sustain, terrain, urbane; appertain, Chamberlain, entertain, hurricane, monoplane, porcelain, scatterbrain, windowpane; legerdemain.

-āint: ain't, faint, feint, mayn't, paint, plaint, quaint, saint, taint; acquaint, attaint, complaint, constraint, depaint, distraint, restraint.

-āir, -āre: air, ayr, bare, bear, blare, care,

5

chair, Claire, Clare, dare, e'er, ere, fair,
fare, flair, flare, gare, glare, hair, hare, heir,
Herr, lair, mare, mayor, pair, pare, pear,
prayer, rare, snare, spare, square, stair,
stare, swear, tare, tear, their, there, they're,
ware, wear, where; affair, armchair, aware,
beware, co-heir, compare, corsair, declare,
despair, eclair, elsewhere, ensnare, fanfare,
forbear, forswear, howe'er, impair, mo-
hair, nightmare, Mayfair, outstare, prepare,
repair, unfair, welfare, whate'er, when-
e'er, where'er; anywhere, commissionaire,
concessionaire, debonair, Delaware, doc-
trinaire, everywhere, millionaire, solitaire,
unaware.

-āise, -āys, -āise, -āze: baize, blaze, braise,
braze, chaise, craze, daze, faze, gaze, glaze,
graze, haze, laze, maize, maze, naze, phase,
phrase, praise, raise, raze, traits, yeas;
ablaze, adaze, amaze, appraise, dispraise;
chrysoprase, Marseillaise, mayonnaise, now-
adays, outgaze, paraphrase, polonaise, self-
praise, upgaze, upraise. (Plurals of -ay,
-ey.)

-āit, -āte, -eight: ait, ate, bait, bate, crate,
date, eight, fate, fete, frate, freight, gait,
gate, grate, great, hate, Kate, late, mate,
Nate, pate, plait, plate, prate, rate, sate,
skate, slate, spate, state, straight, strait,
Tait, trait, wait, weight; abate, aerate,

6

agnate, alate, await, baccate, berate, bookplate. bromate, casemate, castrate, caudate, cerate, checkmate, chelate, collate, cordate, costate, create, cremate, curate, curvate, debate, dilate, donate, elate, equate, estate, falcate, filtrate, frustrate, furcate, gemmate, globate, gradate, gyrate, helpmate, hydrate, inflate, ingrate, inmate, innate, irate, ligate, locate, mandate, migrate, narrate, oblate, orate, ornate, placate, prostrate, sedate, translate, vacate; abdicate, abrogate, acerbate, advocate (verb), aggravate, aggregate, agitate, allocate, amputate, animate, annotate, antedate, antiquate, appellate, arbitrate, arrogate, aspirate, bifurcate, cachinate, calculate, cancellate, candidate, captivate, carbonate, castigate, catenate, celebrate, circulate, cogitate, colligate, compensate, complicate, concentrate, confiscate, conformate, congregate, conjugate, consecrate, constipate, consulate, contemplate, correlate, corrugate, coruscate, crenellate, cultivate, cumulate, cyanate, decimate, decollate, decorate, dedicate, dehydrate, delegate, delicate, demarcate, demonstrate, derogate, desperate, detonate, devastate, dislocate, dissipate, dominate, duplicate, educate, elevate, elongate, emanate, emigrate, emulate, enervate, estimate, excavate, exculpate, extricate, fabricate, fascinate, federate, floriate, formulate, fornicate, generate, germinate, glaciate, gladiate, glomerate, graduate, granulate, gravitate, hesitate, hibernate, imprecate, impregnate, incubate, indicate, indurate, infiltrate, innovate, inoculate, insolate, instigate, insufflate, insulate, integrate, intimate, intonate, intricate, inundate, irrigate, irritate, isolate, iterate, jubilate, lacerate, laminate, laureate, legislate, liquidate, litigate, lubricate, macerate, machinate, magistrate, mediate, medicate, meditate, militate, mitigate, moderate, modulate, mutilate, nauseate, navigate, nominate, nucleate, oscillate, oscitate, osculate, overrate, overstate, penetrate, percolate, perforate, permeate, personate, pollinate, postulate, potentate, predicate, principate, profligate, promulgate, propagate, radiate, radicate, recreate, regulate, relegate, remonstrate, renovate, reprobate, resonate, ruminate, rusticate, satiate, saturate, scintillate, segregate, selenate, separate, simulate, spiflicate, stipulate, subjugate, sublimate, suffocate, sulfurate, syndicate, tabulate, terminate, tete-a-tete, titivate, tolerate, triplicate, triturate, ultimate, umbellate, underrate, understate, underweight, vaccinate, validate, venerate, ventilate, vindicate ; abominate, accelerate, accentuate, accommodate, accumulate, acid-

8

ulate, adulterate, affiliate, agglutinate, alleviate, anticipate, articulate, assassinate, capacitate, coagulate, commemorate, commensurate, commiserate, communicate, compassionate, conciliate, congratulate, consolidate, contaminate, co-operate, coordinate, corroborate, debilitate, deliberate, denominate, depopulate, depreciate, dilapidate, discriminate, ejaculate, elaborate, electorate, eliminate, elucidate, emaciate, equivocate, eradicate, evacuate, expectorate, expostulate, exterminate, facilitate, felicitate, gesticulate, illuminate, immaculate, initiate, inoculate, intimidate, intoxicate, invalidate, investigate, manipulate, matriculate, necessitate, negotiate, participate, precipitate precogitate, preconsulate, predistinate, predominate, premeditate, prevaricate, procrastinate, prognosticate, proliferate, reciprocate, recriminate, recuperate, redecorate, reduplicate, reiterate, reverberate, subordinate, substantiate, syllabicate, transliterate, triumverate, variegate, differentiate, misappropriate, proletariate, rehabilitate, reinvigorate, transsubstantiate. (And many other false rhymes in words ending in -ȧte such as "adequate".)

-āith: faith, Snaith, wraith; misfaith.

-âird: Baird, braird, Caird, laird. (Also preterites of -âir, -āre words.)

-āke: ache, bake, Blake, brake, break, cake, crake, drake, fake, flake, hake, Jake, lake, make, quake, rake, sake, shake, slake, snake, spake, stake, steak, strake, take, wake; awake, backache, bespake, betake, corn crake, forsake, earache, earthquake, heartache, keepsake, mandrake, mistake, namesake, opaque, outbreak, partake, snowflake, sweepstake, toothache, upbreak, uptake; bellyache, johnnycake, overtake, pattycake, rattlesnake, undertake.

-al: Al, chal (Romany), Hal, mal, pal, Sal, shall; banal, cabal, canal, corral, locale, morale, Natal, timbale; musicale; Guadalcanal. (And more than 100 false rhymes in words ending in **-àl** in which the final syllable is not accented, such as "animal".)

-äl: Transvaal. (See **-ärl**.)

-alc: talc; catafalque.

-äld: bald, scald; Archibald, piebald, so-called. (See preterites of verbs ending in **-ăll**, **-ăul**, and **-ăwl**.)

-āle: See **-āil**.

-alf: See **-aff**.

-ălk, -ăuk, ăwk: auk, balk, calk, caulk, chalk, gawk, hawk, squawk, stalk, talk, walk; catwalk, Dundalk, Mohawk, tomahawk. (See **-ôrk**.)

10

-älm: alm, balm, calm, Guam, palm, psalm, qualm, becalm, embalm, madame, salaam.

-äll, -äul, -äwl: all, awl, ball, brawl, call, caul, crawl, drawl, fall, gall, Gaul, hall, haul, mall, maul, pall, Paul, pawl, Saul, scrawl, shawl, small, sprawl, squall, stall, tall, thrall, trawl, wall, yawl; appall, befall, Bengal, baseball, catcall, enthrall, football, footfall, install, Nepal, rainfall, snowfall, Whitehall, windfall; basketball, overhaul, waterfall; wherewithal.

-alp: alp, Alp, palp, scalp.

-ält, -ault: fault, halt, malt, salt, smalt, vault; asphalt, assault, basalt, cobalt, default, exalt; somersault.

-alve (silent L): calve, halve, have, salve. (See -ärve.)

-alve (L sounded): salve, valve; bivalve.

-am: am, Cam, Cham, clam, cram, dam, damn, drachm, dram, flam, gam, gram, ham, jam, jamb, lam, lamb, mam, pam, pram, ram, Sam, scram, sham, slam, swam, tram, wham, yam; Assam, flimflam, madame, Siam. (And many false rhymes including bantam, bedlam, cryptogram.)

-äme: See -äim.

-amp: amp. camp, champ, clamp, cramp, damp, gamp, lamp, ramp, samp, scamp,

11

stamp, tamp, tramp, vamp; decamp, encamp, enstamp, firedamp, revamp; safetylamp, signal lamp. (For rhymes to "swamp", see -omp.)

-an: an, Ann, Anne, ban, bran, can, clan, Dan, fan, flan, Fran, Jan, khan, man, Nan, pan, Pan, plan, ran, scan, span, tan, than, van; Afghan, began, corban, divan, fireman, foreran, inspan, Iran, Koran, merman, Milan, outran, outspan, pavan, pecan, rattan, redan, Sedan, trepan, unman; artisan, barbican, barracan, caravan, Castellan, charlatan, clergyman, countryman, courtesan, fisherman, fugleman, Indian, juryman, Mexican, Michigan, midshipman, nobleman, Ottoman, overran, pelican, puritan, superman, Thespian, talisman. (And about 100 false rhymes in words in which the final syllable is not accentuated, such as "African".) For rhymes to "swan," see -on.

-ance, -anse: chance, dance, France, glance, lance, manse, prance, stance, trance; advance, askance, bechance, enhance, entrance, expanse, finance, mischance, perchance, puissance, romance, seance; circumstance; extravagance. (And about 30 false rhymes in words ending in -ance in which the final syllable is not accentuated, such as "ambulance", "vigilance", etc.)

12

-anch: blanch, Blanche, branch, flanch, ganch, ranch, scranch, stanch; carteblanche; avalanche.

-anct: sacrosanct. (Extend **-ank + ed** as in spanked, cranked.)

-and: and, band, bland, brand, gland, grand, hand, land, manned, rand, Rand, sand, stand, Strand, strand; command, demand, disband, expand, imband, remand, unhand, unland, withstand; contraband, countermand, fairy-land, fatherland, firebrand, hinterland, Holy Land, overland, reprimand, Rio Grande, saraband, Sunderland, understand, upper-hand, wonderland. (And preterites of verbs ending in **-an.** For rhymes to "wand", see **-ond.**)

-āne: See **-āin.**

-ang: bang, bhang, clang, fang, gang, gangue, hang, Lang, pang, rang, sang, slang, spang, sprang, stang, swang, tang, twang, whang, yang; harangue, meringue, mustang, orang-outang, Penang, serang, shebang, trepang, uphang; boomerang, overhang.

-ānge: change, grange, mange, range, strange; arrange, derange, enrange, estrange, exchange; disarrange, interchange, rearrange.

-ank: bank, blank, brank, chank, clank,

crank, dank, drank, flank, franc, frank,
Frank, hank, lank, plank, prank, rank,
sank, shank, shrank, slank, spank, stank,
swank, tank, thank, twank, yank, Yank;
embank, enrank, disrank, mountebank, out-
flank, outrank, point-blank; savings-bank.

-ant: ant, aunt, bant, brant, can't, cant,
chant, grant, Grant, Kant, pant, plant,
rant, scant, shan't, slant; aslant, decant,
descant, displant, enchant, extant, gallant,
implant, Levant, recant, supplant, trans-
plant; adamant, commandant, disenchant,
gallivant, heirophant. (And about 50 false
rhymes by wrongly accentuating the final
syllable of such words as "arrogant", etc.
For rhymes to "want", see ônt.)

-anx: francs, Lancs, Manx. (And pluralize
words ending in -ank.)

-ap: cap, chap, clap, dap, flap, frap, gap,
hap, Jap, knap, lap, map, nap, pap, rap,
sap, scrap, slap, snap, strap, tap, trap,
wrap, yap; bestrap, claptrap, entrap, en-
wrap, kidnap, madcap, mayhap, mishap,
nightcap, unwrap; afterclap, handicap,
overlap, rattletrap, thunderclap.

-āpe: ape, cape, Cape, chape, crape, dape,
drape, gape, grape, jape, nape, rape,
scrape, shape, tape, trape; agape, escape,
landscape, red-tape, seascape, ship-shape,

14

transshape, uncape, unshape.

-āpes: traipse, jackanapes. (And add "s" to the above.)

-aph: See -aff.

-apse: apse, craps, lapse, schnapps; collapse, elapse, illapse, perhaps, relapse; interlapse, after-claps. (And add "s" to words under -ap.)

-aque: See -ack.

-är: Aar, are, bar, car, char, czar, dar, far, jar, knar, Loire, mar, par, parr, Saar, scar, spar, star, tar, tsar; afar, ajar, bazaar, bizarre, catarrh, cigar, cymar, daystar, debar, disbar, embar, feldspar, guitar, horsecar, hussar, instar, jaguar, Lascar, Navarre, pourboire, unbar, upbar; Calabar, calendar, cinnabar, circular, consular, globular, insular, Malabar, modular, ocular, registrar, regular, scapular, secular, seminar, similar, tabular, vinegar, Zanzibar.

-ärb: barb, garb, yarb; rhubarb.

-ärce, -ärse: carse, farce, parse, sparse. (For rhymes to "parse", pluralize some words in -är.)

-ärch: arch, larch, march, March, parch, starch; outmarch; countermarch, overarch, overmarch.

-ärd: bard, card, chard, guard, hard, lard,

nard, pard, sard, **shard**, yard; Bernard, bombard, canard, **closebarred**, discard, **enguard**, foulard, Girard, life-guard, petard, **placard**, regard, retard, unguard, unmarred; afterguard, avant-garde, bodyguard, boulevard, disregard, interlard, leotard, poultry-yard. (Extend -är for "barred" and other preterites. For rhymes to "ward", see -ôard.)

-äre (as in "rare"): See -air.

-ärf: corf, dwarf, wharf; endomorph, mesomorph.

-ärge: barge, charge, Farge, large, marge, sparge, targe; discharge, enlarge, litharge, surcharge, uncharge; overcharge, supercharge, undercharge.

-ärk: arc, ark, bark, barque, cark, clerk, dark, hark, knark, lark, marc, mark, Mark, marque, nark, park, Sark, shark, "Snark", spark, stark, Starke; aardvark, bedark, debark, dispark, embark, hierarch, landmark, remark, tanbark; disembark, hierarch, matriarch, oligarch, patriarch.

-ärl, -äal: Basle, carl, Carl, gnarl, marl, snarl; ensnarl, imparl; Albemarle.

-ärm: arm, barm, charm, farm, harm, marm, smarm; alarm, disarm, forearm, gendarme, schoolmarm, unarm. (For rhymes to "warm", see ôrm.)

-ärn: barn, darn, "garn", Larne, Marne,

tarn, yarn; incarn. (For rhymes to "warn", see -ôrn.)

-ärp: carp, harp, scarp, sharp, Zarp; counterscarp, epicarp, monocarp, pericarp.

-ärse: farce, parse, sparse. (And add "s" to words in -är.)

-ärsh: harsh, marsh.

-ärt: art, bart, cart, chart, dart, hart, heart, mart, part, smart, start, tart; apart, depart, dispart, impart, rampart, sweetheart, upstart; counterpart.

-art: See -ort.

-ärve: carve, larve, starve. (See -alve.)

-as, -azz: as, has, jazz, "razz"; LaPaz.

-äse: See -äce.

-ash: ash, bash, brash, cache, cash, clash, crash, dash, fash (Scotch), flash, gash, gnash, hash, lache, lash, mash, Nash, pash, plash, rash, sash, slash, smash, splash, tache, thrash, trash; abash, calash, moustache, panache, Wabash; balderdash, calabash, sabretache, succotash.

-äsh: quash, squash, wash; goulash, musquash; mackintosh, mishmash. (And slang words as follows: Boche, bosh, cosh, gosh, josh, posh, slosh, splosh, tosh.)

-ask: ask, bask, Basque, cask, casque, flask,

mask, task; bemask, unmask, overtask, water-cask.

-asm: chasm, plasm, spasm; miasm, orgasm, phantasm, sarcasm; cataplasm, pleonasm, protoplasm; enthusiasm, iconoclasm.

-asp: asp, clasp, gasp, grasp, hasp, rasp; enclasp, engrasp, unclasp.

-ass: ass, bass, brass, class, crass, gas, glass, grass, lass, mass, pass; alas, amass, crevasse, cuirasse, culrass, harass, impass, Madras, morass, paillasse, repass, surpass; unclass; coup-de-grace, demitasse, hippocras, looking glass, sassafras, underpass.

-ast: bast, blast, cast, caste, fast, gassed, hast, last, massed, mast, past, vast; aghast, avast, bombast, contrast, cuitassed, downcast, forecast, handfast, outcast, peltast, repast, steadfast, unfast; elegiast, metaplast, paraphrast ; ecclesiast, enthusiast, flabbergast, iconoclast. (And preterites of **-ass** words.)

-āste: baste, chaste, haste, paste, taste, waist, waste ; distaste, foretaste, impaste, lambaste, unchaste ; aftertaste. (And preterites of many **-āce** and **-āse** words.)

-at: at, bat, brat, cat, chat, drat, fat, flat, "gat", gnat, hat, Jat, mat, Matt, Nat, pat, Pat, plait, plat, Platte, rat, sat, scat, slat, spat, sprat, tat, that, vat; combat, cravat, hellcat, Herat, loquat, polecat, whereat, wombat; acrobat, autocrat, automat, democrat, diplomat, habitat, hemostat, photostat, plutocrat, thermostat, tit for tat; aristocrat, Montserrat.

-āte: See -āit.

-atch: See -ach.

path, "rath" (Carroll), scath, wrath; bypath; aftermath, allopath, philomath, psychopath; homeopath, osteopath, physiopath.

-āthe: bathe, lathe, scathe, snathe, spathe, swathe; unswathe.

-ăub, -ôrb: daub, orb, Taube; adsorb.

-ăud: bawd, broad, Claude, fraud, gaud, laud, Maud; abroad, applaud, belaud, defraud, maraud. (And many preterites of verbs on -aw, as "clawed". See -ôard and -ôrde.)

-augh: See -aff.

-ăught, -ôught: aught, bought, brought, caught, fought, fraught, naught, nought, ought, sought, taught, taut, thought, wrought; besought, bethought, Connaught, distraught, dreadnought, forethought, methought, onslaught; aeronaut, afterthought, Argonaut, astronaut, juggernaut, overwrought. (See -ôrt.)

-ăuk, ăulk, -awk: See -alk.

-ăun: See -ăwn.

19

-äunch: craunch, haunch, launch, paunch, staunch.

-äunt: aunt, chaunt, daunt, flaunt, gaunt, haunt, jaunt, taunt, vaunt, want; avaunt, romaunt.

-äuse, -äuze: awes, cause, clause, gauze, hawse, pause, tawse, yaws; applause, because, turquoise. (And add "s" to certain words in **-aw.**)

-äv: have, Slav, sauve (compare **-alve.**)

-äve: brave, cave, crave, Dave, drave, frave, gave, Glaive, grave, knave, lave, nave, pave, rave, save, shave, slave, stave, suave, they've, trave, waive, wave; behave, concave, conclave, deprave, engrave, enslave, exclave, forgave, impave, margrave, misgave, outbrave, ungrave; misbehave.

-äw: awe, caw, chaw, claw, craw, daw, draw, faugh, flaw, gnaw, haw, jaw, law, maw, paw, pshaw, raw, saw, Shaw, squaw, straw, taw, thaw, yaw; cat's-paw, Choctaw, coleslaw, foresaw, guffaw, jackdaw, jigsaw, macaw, papaw, seesaw, southpaw, Warsaw, withdraw; Arkansas, overawe, usquebaugh

-äwk: See **-älk.**

-äwl: See **-äll.**

-äwn: awn, bawn, brawn, dawn, drawn, faun, fawn, gone, lawn, pawn, prawn, sawn, Sean, spawn, yawn; indrawn. (See **-orn.**)

20

-ax: ax, claques, flax, lax, Max, pax, plaques, sax (for saxophone), **tax, wax, zax**; addax, Ajax, anthrax, borax, **climax, relax,** syntax, thorax; Analax, battle-ax, **Halifax,** parallax. (See -ac and -ack and add "s".)

-az: **as,** has, jazz, razz; whereas. (See -as.)

-āze: See -āise.

-āste: baste, chaste, haste, paste, taste, waist, waste; distaste, foretaste, impaste, **lambaste, unchaste; aftertaste. (Also preterites of -ace and -ase words.)**

-āy, -ey, -eigh: a, aye, bay, bey, brae, **bray,** Bray, clay, day, dray, drey, eh, fay, **Fay,** fey, flay, fray, gay, gray, greige, grey, **hay,** jay, Kay, lay, lah, Mae, may, May, **nay,** née, neigh, pay, play, pray, prey, ray, **Ray,** say, shay, slay, sleigh, spay, spray, **stay,** stray, sway, Tay, they, tray, trey, **way,** weigh, whey, yea; abbé, affray, **agley,** allay, array, assay, astray, away, belay, beret, betray, bewray, Bombay, bouquet, cabaret, café, Calais, Cathay, causeway, chambray, convey, coupé, croquet, curé, decay, defray, delay, dismay, display, doomsday, dragée, embay, endplay, essay, filet, foray, foyer, Friday, gainsay, gangway, hearsay, Herne Bay, heyday, hooray, horseplay, inlay, inveigh, Malay, Manet, melee, mid-day, mislay, Moray,

21

Monday, Monet, nosegay, obey, okay, ole!,
passé, per se, portray, prepay, purée, purvey, relay, repay, replay, risqué, Roget,
roué, sachet, sashay, soirée, soufflé, sub-
way, Sunday, survey, throughway, Thurs-
day, today, tokay, touché, toupée, Tuesday,
waylay, Wednesday; appliqué, cabaret,
canapé, castaway, Chevrolet, consommé,
disarray, disobey, émigré, exposé, holiday,
matinée, Monterey, negligée, popinjay, pro-
tégé, résumé, runaway, Santa Fe, Saturday,
sobriquet, stowaway, yesterday; Appian
Way, cabriolet, communiqué, habitué. (And
more than 30 false rhymes, such as "high-
way", "Monday", "popinlay", etc.)

-ē, ēa, ēe: be, bee, Cree, Dee, dree, fee, flea,
flee, free, gee, ghee, glee, he, key, knee, lea,
lee, Lee, Leigh, ley, li, me, "oui", pea, plea,
quay, rhe, scree, sea, see, she, si, ski, snee,
spree, Spree, tea, tee, thee, three, tree, we,
wee, ye; agree, alee, bailee, banshee, bargee,
bohea, bootie, coo-ee, debris, decree, degree, donee, drawee, Dundee, esprit, fäerie,
fusee, grandee, grantee, jinnee, kildee, les-
see, levee, M.D., McGee, mustee, "on dit",
Parsee, payee, pledgee, pongee, pontee, raki,
rani, rupee, settee, squeegee, suttee, tehee,
Torquay, trustee, vendee, vouchee; absentee,
addressee, advowee, allottee, alshantee, as-
signee, avowee, baloney, botany, bourgeoisie,

bumblebee, calorie, cap-a-pie, Cherokee,
chickadee, chimpanzee, consignee, coterie,
debauchee, devotee, disagree, divorcee, dun-
garee, fricasee, Galilee, garnishee, guaran-
tee, harmony, honey-bee, hyperbole, irony,
jamboree, Japanee, jeu d'esprit, jubilee,
legatee, licensee, Lombardy, manatee, mort-
gagee, nominee, Normandy, oversea, pat-
entee, pedigree, Pharisee, pugaree, recipe,
referee, refugee, releasee, remittee, repar-
tee, Sadducee, scarabee, selvagee, simile,
symphony, systole, third degree, tyranny,
unforesee, vertebrae, warrantee, whiffletree;
abalone, anemone, apostrophe, Antigone,
Ariadne, calliope, catastrophe, facsimile,
hyperbole, macarone, Penelope, synonymy.

-ēace, -ēase: cease, crease, creese, fleece,
geese, grease, Greece, lease, Nice, niece,
peace, piece; apiece, caprice, cerise, Clarice, decease, decrease, Felice, increase,
Lucrece, Maurice, obese, police, release,
surcease, Therese, valise; afterpiece, am-
bergris, battlepiece, cantatrice, frontispiece,
mantelpiece, masterpiece.

-ēach: beach, beech, bleach, breach, breech,
each, leech, peach, preach, reach, screech,
speech, teach; beseech, impeach, outreach,
unbreech, unpreach; overreach.

-ead: See -ed.

-ead, -ede, -eed: bead, Bede, bleed, breed, cede, creed, deed, feed, freed, glebe, greed, heed, keyed, knead, lead, mead, Mede, meed, need, plead, read, reed, screed, seed, speed, steed, swede, Swede, teed, tweed, Tweed, weed; accede, agreed, concede, decreed, exceed, impede, indeed, knock-kneed, linseed, misdeed, mislead, precede, proceed, recede, refereed, secede, stampede, succeed; antecede, centipede, filigreed, Ganymede, guaranteed, intercede, millipede, overfeed, supersede; velocipede.

-eaf, -ef: chef, clef, deaf, Jeff; Khrushchev.

-eaf: See -eef.

-eague, -igue: Greig, league, teague; colleague, enleague, fatigue, intrigue.

-eak, -eek, -ique: beak, bleak, cheek, chic, cleek, clique, creak, creek, eke, freak, Greek, leak, leek, meek, peak, peek, pique, reek, seek, sheik, shriek, Sikh, sleek, sneak, speak, squeak, streak, teak, tweak, weak, week, wreak; aleak, antique, apeak, bespeak, bezique, critique, forespeak, oblique, physique, relique, unique, unspeak, upseek; Chesapeake, Frederique, Martinique, Mozambique, Pathétique.

-eal, -eel: ceil, creel, deal, Deal, eel, feel, heal, heel, he'll, keel, Kiel, kneel, leal, meal, Neal, Neil, peal, peel, real, reel, seal, she'll,

skeel, spiel, squeal, steal, steel, streel, sweal,
teal, veal, weal, we'll, wheel, zeal; anele,
anneal, appeal, Bastille, cartwheel, Castille,
chenille, conceal, congeal, genteel, ideal,
Lucille, misdeal, mobile, pastille, repeal, re-
veal, unreal; cochineal, commonweal, des-
habille, mercantile; automobile.

-ēald, -iēld: field, shield, weald, wield, yield;
afield, enshield; battlefield, Chesterfield.
(And preterites of verbs in previous list.)

-ealm: elm, heim, realm, whelm; overwhelm,

-ealth: health, stealth, wealth; common-
wealth.

-ēam, -ēem: beam, bream, Cheam, cream,
deem, dream, fleam, gleam, ream, scheme,
scream, seam, seem, steam, stream, team,
teem, theme; abeam, beseem, blaspheme,
centime, daydream, esteem, extreme, ice
cream, moonbeam, redeem, regime, supreme,
unseam, unteam; disesteem, self-esteem.

-eamt, -empt: dreamt, kempt, tempt; attempt,
contempt, exempt, pre-empt, unkempt.

-ēan, -ēen: bean, been, clean, dean, Deane,
e'en, Gene, glean, green, Jean, jean, keen,
lean, lien, mean, mesne, mien, quean,
queen, scene, screen, seen, sheen, spleen,
teen, wean, ween, yean; advene, atween,
baleen, beguine, between, canteen, careen,
chlorine, Christine, codeine, convene, cui-

25

sine, demean, demesne, Doreen, eighteen,
Eileen, Eugene, fifteen, foreseen, fourteen,
Kathleen, machine, MacLean, marine, nine-
teen, obscene, Pauline, poteen, praline, pro-
tein, quinine, ravine, routine, sardine, se-
rene, shagreen, sixteen, sordine, spalpeen,
subvene, terrene, tontine, tureen, umpteen,
unclean, unseen, zebrine ; Aberdeen, Abi-
lene, aniline, Argentine, atabrine, bomba-
zine, brigantine, contravene, crinoline,
damascene, evergreen, Florentine, gabar-
dine, Geraldine, gelatine, go-between, guil-
lotine, indigene, intervene, Jacqueline, ker-
osene, magazine, mezzanine, Nazarene, nec-
tarine, nicotine, overseen, quarantine, saccharine, seccotine, serpentine, seventeen,
submarine, tambourine, tangerine, unfore-
seen, vaseline, velvetine, wolverine; aqua-
marine, elephantine, ultramarine.

-ēand, -iēnd: fiend. (And preterites of some
verbs in previous list.)

-eant: See -ent.

-ēap, -ēep: cheap, cheep, chepe, clepe, creep,
deep, heap, jeep, keep, leap, neap, peep,
reap, seep, sheep, sleep, steep, sweep,
threap, weep; asleep, beweep, overleap.

-ēar, -ēer, -ēir, -ēre, -iēr: beer, bier, blear,
cere, cheer, clear, dear, deer, drear, ear,
fear, fleer, gear, hear, Heer, here, jeer,

lear, leer, meer, mere, mir, near, peer, pier, queer, rear, sear, seer, sere, shear, sheer, "skeer", smear, sneer, spear, sphere, steer, tear, tier, vere, veer, weir, year; adhere, appear, arrear, austere, besmear, career, cashier, Cashmere, cohere, compeer, emir, endear, fakir, frontier, inhere, insphere, madrier, rehear, reindeer, revere, severe, sincere, Tangier, uprear, veneer; atmosphere, auctioneer, bandoleer, bombardier, brigadier, buccaneer, carabineer, cannoneer, cavalier, chandelier, chanticleer, chevalier, chiffonier, commandeer, disappear, domineer, engineer, fusilier, gazetteer, gondolier, grenadier, halberdier, hemisphere, insincere, interfere, mountaineer, muleteer, musketeer, mutineer, overhear, overseer, pamphleteer, persevere, pioneer, privateer, profiteer, scrutineer, sonneteer, volunteer, Windemere.

-êarch, -êrch, -îrch, ûrch: birch, church, Kertch, lurch, perch, search, smirch; besmirch, research.

-eard (short), **-erd, -ird, -urd:** bird, curd, gird, heard, herd, Kurd, shirred, surd, third, word; absurd, blackbird, lovebird, songbird, ungird, unheard; hummingbird, ladybird, mockingbird, overheard; unsepulchred. (And preterites of many verbs in -êr, îr, and ûr words.)

27

-ēard (long), -ēird: beard, tiered, weird;
   afeard. (And more than 40 preterites of
   -ear, -eer, -ere.)

-êarl, îrl, -ûrl: Beryl, burl, churl, curl, earl,
   furl, girl, hurl, jurl, knurl, pearl, purl,
   skirl, swirl, twirl, whirl, whorl; uncurl,
   unfurl.

-êarled, îrled, -orld: world. (And preterites
   of verbs in previous list.)

-êarn, -êrn, -ûrn: Berne, burn, churn, earn,
   erne, fern, hern, kern, learn, querne, spurn,
   stern, tern, turn, urn, yearn; adjourn,
   astern, concern, discern, eterne, intern, Lu-
   cerne, return, sojourn, unlearn; overturn,
   taciturn, unconcern.

-êarse: See -êrce.

-eärt: See -art.

-êarth, -êrth, îrth: berth, birth, dearth,
   earth, firth, girth, mirth, Perth, worth;
   stillbirth, unearth.

-ēase (as in "lease"): See -ēace.

-ēase, -ēz, -ēeze, -ise: bise, breeze, cheese,
   ease, freeze, frieze, Guise, grease (verb),
   he's, lees, mise, pease, please, seize, she's,
   skis, sneeze, squeeze, tease, these, wheeze;
   appease, Bernice, Burmese, cerise, chemise,
   Chinese, disease, displease, Louise, Maltese,
   Thales, trapeze, valise; ABC's, Achilles,

Androcles, antifreeze, Antilles, Balinese,
Cantonese, Hercules, Japanese, Javanese,
journalese, obsequies, overseas, Pekingese,
Portuguese, Siamese, Tyrolese, Viennese.
(And plurals of -ē, -ēa, -ēe.)

-ēast, -iēst: beast, east, feast, least, priest,
yeast; artiste. (And preterites of -ēace and
-ēace and -ēase (-ēz).)

-ēat, -ēet, -ēit, -ite: beat, beet, bleat, cheat,
cleat, Crete, eat, feat, feet, fleet, greet, heat,
meat, meet, mete, neat, peat, Pete, pleat,
seat, sheet, skeet, sleet, street, suite, sweet,
teat, treat, wheat; accrete, aesthete, afreet,
athlete, compete, complete, conceit, con-
crete, deceit, defeat, delete, deplete, dis-
creet, discrete, effete, elite, entreat, escheat,
petite, receipt, repeat, replete, retreat, se-
crete; bittersweet, Easy Street, incomplete,
indiscreet, obsolete, overeat, parakeet, sun-
ny-sweet, winding-sheet. (For rhymes to
"great", see -āit.)

-eath (eth): Beth, breath, death, saith, Seth;
Macbeth; Elizabeth, twentieth.

-ēath: heath, Keith, Meath, 'neath, Neath,
sheath, teeth, wreath; beneath, bequeath,
Blackheath, Dalkeith, unsheathe; under-
neath.

-ēathe: breathe, seethe, sheathe, sneathe,
teethe, wreathe; bequeathe, ensheath, en-

29

wreathe, inbreathe, unsheathe, upbreathe.

-ēave, -ēive, -ēve, -iēve: beeve, breve, cleave, deev, eave, eve, Eve, greave, grieve, heave, keeve, leave, lieve, peeve, reave, reeve, screeve, seave, sheave, sleave, sleeve, Steeve, Steve, thieve, vive, weave, we've; achieve, aggrieve, believe, bereave, conceive, deceive, perceive, receive, relieve, reprieve, retrieve, unreave, unreeve, unweave, upheave; Christmas-eve, disbelieve, interweave, misconceive.

-eaw: See **-ōw.**

-eb, -ebb: bleb, deb, ebb, Feb., neb, reb, web; sub-deb.

-eck: beck, check, cheque, Czech, deck, fleck, "heck", neck, peck, reck, sec, speck, tech, trek, wreck; bedeck, bewreck, henpeck, Quebec, zebec; Kennebec, leatherneck, neck-and-neck, quarter-deck.

-ect: sect; abject, adject, affect, bisect, collect, conflict, connect, correct, defect, deflect, deject, detect, direct, dissect, effect, eject, elect, erect, expect, infect, inject, insect, inspect, neglect, object, pandect, perfect, prefect, project, prospect, protect, reflect, reject, respect, select, subject, suspect, traject; architect, circumspect, dialect, disaffect, disconnect, disinfect, disrespect, incorrect, intellect, interject, intersect, in-

30

trospect, misdirect, non-elect, recollect, re-
trospect, self-respect, unsuspect. (And preterites of -eck words.)

-ed, -ead (short): bed, bled, bread, bred, dead,
dread, Ed, fed, fled, Fred, head, lead, led,
Ned, pled, read, red, said, shed, shred,
sled, sped, spread, stead, Ted, thread, tread,
wed, zed; abed, ahead, behead, bestead,
biped, blockhead, bulkhead, coed, hogshead,
inbred, instead, misled, outspread, unread,
unsaid; aforesaid, gingerbread, loggerhead,
quadruped, thoroughbred, thunder-head,
timber-head, trucklebed, underfed, water-
shed, Winifred. (And endings in -ed when
accentuated, as in "visited.")

-ēde: See -ēad.

-edge: dredge, edge, fledge, hedge, kedge,
ledge, pledge, Reg (for Reginald), sedge,
sledge, veg. (for vegetables), wedge; al-
lege, enhedge, impledge, unedge; inter-
pledge, privilege, sacrilege.

-ēe: See ē.

-ēece: See -ēace.

-ēech: See -ēach.

-ēed: See -ēad.

-ēef, -iēf: beef, brief, chief, fief, feoff, grief,
leaf, lief, reef, sheaf, thief; belief, fig leaf,

31

relief, shereef, bas relief, disbelief, enfeoff, handkerchief, interleaf, neckerchief, unbelief; aperitif.

-ēek: See -ēak.

-ēel: See -ēal.

-ēem: See -ēam.

-ēer: See -ēar.

-ēese: See -ēase.

-ēet: See -ēat.

-eft: cleft, deft, eft, heft, left, reft, theft, weft; aleft, bereft; enfeoffed, unbereft.

-eg: beg, clegg, dreg, egg, keg, leg, Meg, peg, Peg, seg, skeg, teg, yegg; nutmeg, pegleg, unpeg; beglerbeg, philabeg, Winnipeg.

-egm: See -em.

-eigh: See -āy

-eign, -ein: See -āin.

-el, -elle: bel, bell, belle, cell, dell, dwell, El, ell, fell, hell, jell, knell, Nell, pell, quell, sell, shell, smell, snell, spell, swell, tell, well, yell, Zel, Zell; befell, compel, Cornell, debel, dispel, Estelle, excel, expel, farewell, foretell, gazelle, harebell, hotel, impel, inshell, lapel, pell-mell, propell, Purnell, rebel, repel, rondelle, sea-shell, sentinel, unshell, unspell; asphodel, Astrophel, A.W.O.L., bagatelle, bechamel, calomel, caramel, citadel, cockerel, demoiselle, div-

32

ing-bell, doggerel, immortelle, infidel, Lionel, mackerel, muscatel, nonpareil, parallel, personnel, pimpernel, philomel, sentinel, undersell, vesper-bell, villanelle; mademoiselle.

-elch: belch, squelch, Welch, Welsh.

-eld: eld, geld, held, meld, weld; beheld, unknelled, upheld, unquelled, withheld; unbeheld; unparalleled. (And preterites of -el words.)

-elf: delf, delph, elf, Guelph, pelf, self, shelf; herself, himself, itself, myself, ourself, thyself, yourself.

-elk: elk, whelk, yelk.

-elm: See -ealm.

-elp: help, kelp, skelp, swelp, whelp, yelp; self-help.

-elt: belt, Celt, dealt, dwelt, felt, gelt, Kelt, knelt, melt, pelt, smelt, spelt, svelte, veldt, welt; heart-felt, misspelt, unbelt, unfelt.

-elve: delve, helve, shelve, twelve.

-em: em, femme, gem, hem, Jem, phlegm, Shem, stem, them; ahem, begem, condemn, contemn, pro tem; apothegm, Bethlehem, diadem, requiem, stratagem, theorem; ad hominem.

-ēme: See -ēam.

-emp: hemp, kemp.

-empt: See **-eampt.**

-en: Ben, den, fen, glen, Gwen, hen, ken, men, pen, sen, ten, then, wen, when, wren, yen, zen; again, amen, cayenne, Cheyenne, Darien, sen-sen, unpen; aldermen, brevipen, cyclamen, denizen, halogen, hydrogen, nitrogen, oxygen, regimen, specimen, waterhen; comedienne, equestrienne, Parisienne, tragedienne.

-ence, -ense: cense, dense, fence, hence, pence, sense, tense, thence, whence; commence, condense, defense, dispense, expense, Hortense, immense, incense, intense, offense, prepense, pretense, suspense, abstinence, accidence, affluence, ambience, audience, commonsense, competence, conference, confidence, consequence, continence, difference, diffidence, diligence, eloquence, eminence, evidence, excellence, frankincense, immanence, imminence, impotence, impudence, incidence, indigence, inference, influence, innocence, insolence, negligence, opulence, penitence, permanence, pertinence, pestilence, preference, prevalence, prominence, recompense, redolence, reference, residence, resilience, sapience, succulence, truculence, turbulence, vehemence, violence, virulence; beneficence, benevolence, circumference, grandiloquence, inconsequence, intelligence, intransigence,

34

magnificence, munificence, obedience, omnipotence, preeminence, subservience. (Also ent + s as in "tents.")

-ench: bench, blench, clench, drench, flench, French, quench, stench, tench, trench, wench, wrench; intrench, retrench, unclench; monkey-wrench.

-end: bend, blend, end, fend, friend, kenned, lend, mend, penned, rend, send, spend, tend, trend, vend, wend; amend, append, ascend, attend, befriend, commend, contend, defend, depend, descend, distend, expend, extend, forfend, impend, intend, misspend, offend, Ostend, perpend, portend, pretend, South End, subtend, suspend, transcend, unbend, unfriend, unkened, unpenned, upend, upsend; apprehend, comprehend, condescend, dividend, minuend, recommend, reprehend, subtrahend; overextend, superintend.

-ength: length, strength; full-length.

-ens: cleanse, ens, lens. (Also **-en** + s as in "pens" and **-end** + s as in "trends".)

-ense: See **-ence.**

-ent, -ént: bent, blent, cent, dent, fent, gent, Ghent, Kent, leant, lent, Lent, meant, pent, rent, scent, sent, spent, tent, Trent, vent, went; absent (verb), accent (verb), anent, ascent, assent, augment, cement, comment, consent, content, descent, dissent, event, extent, ferment, forment, frequent, indent, intent, invent, lament, lenient, misspent, ostent, portent, present (verb), prevent, relent, repent, resent, torment, unbent, unspent; abstinent, accident, ailment, argument, armament, banishment, battlement, betterment, blandishment, blazonment, blemishment, botherment, chastisement, competent, complement, compliment, condiment, confident, confluent, consequent, continent, corpulent, dazzlement, decrement, deferent, detriment, different, diffident, diligent, discontent, dissident, document, element, eloquent, eminent, emollient, esculent, evident, excellent, exigent, filament, firmament, fosterment, fraudulent, government, gradient, immanent, imminent, implement, impotent, impudent, incident, increment, indigent, indolent, innocent, insolent, instrument, languishment, lavishment, liniment, malcontent, management, measurement, merriment, miscontent, monument, negligent, nourishment, nutriment, occident, opulent, orient, ornament, parliament, pediment, penitent, permanent, pertinent, precedent, president, prevalent, prisonment, provident, punishment, ravishment, redolent, regiment, represent, resident, reticent, reverent, rudiment, sacra-

ment, sediment, sentiment, settlement, sub-
sequent, succulent, supplement, tenement,
testament, truculent, turbulent, underwent,
vehement, violent, virulent, wonderment;
accomplishment, acknowledgment, adver-
tisement, astonishment, belligerent, benev-
olent, development, disarmament, embar-
rassment, embodiment, enlightenment,
environment, establishment, experiment,
impenitent, impertinent, imprisonment, im-
provident, intelligent, irreverent, magnifi-
cent, magniloquent, predicament, presenti-
ment, replenishment, subservient, tempera-
ment; accompaniment. (Also see -ant.)

-epp: hep, nep, pep, "prep", rep, repp, skep,
step, steppe, yep; Dieppe, footstep, demirep;
Amenhotep. (Pluralize to rhyme with
"Schweppes" and "steppes".)

-ept: crept, drept, kept, lept, leapt, pepped,
Sept, slept, stepped, swept, wept; accept,
adept, concept, except, inept, precept, un-
kept, unwept, y-clept; intercept, overslept,
overstepped.

-êr, ûr, îr: blur, bur, burr, cur, err, fir,
fur, her, knur, myrrh, per, purr, shirr, sir,
slur, spur, stir, were, whir; astir, aver,
Ben Hur, bestir, Big Sur, chasseur,
chauffeur, coiffeur, concur, confer, defer,
demur, deter, douceur, hauteur, incur, in-

fer, inter, occur, prefer, recur, refer, transfer; amateur, arbiter, barrister, calendar, chronicler, chorister, colander, comforter, connoisseur, cylinder, de rigueur, disinter, doughtier, dowager, drowsier, earlier, gossamer, harbinger, huskier, Jennifer, Jupiter, lavender, Lucifer, mariner, massacre, messenger, minister, officer, passenger, prisoner, register, scimitar, sepulcher, traveler, voyageur; administer, astrologer, astronomer, barometer, Excalibur, idolater, practitioner, relinquisher, thermometer, topographer, upholsterer, worshipper.

-êrb, ûrb: blurb, curb, herb, kerb, Serb, verb; ascerb, adverb, disturb, perturb, suburb, superb.

-êrce, -êrse, -ûrse: curse, Erse, hearse, herse, nurse, purse, terse, verse, worse; accurse, adverse, amerce, asperse, averse, coerce, commerce, converse, disburse, disperse, diverse, imburse, immerse, inverse, obverse, preverse, precurse, rehearse, reverse, sesterce, subcerse, traverse, transverse, intersperse, reimburse, universe.

-êrd: See -êard.

-êre: See -êar.

-êrf, ûrf: scurf, serf, turf.

-êrge, -îrge, -ûrge, -oûrge: dirge, gurge, merge, purge, scourge, serge, splurge,

Spurge, surge, urge, verge; converge, de-
terge, diverge, emerge, immerge, submerge;
demuirge, dramaturge, thaumaturge.

-êrk, -îrk, -ûrk: Burke, Chirk, cirque, clerk,
dirk, irk, jerk, kirk, lurk, merk, murk,
perk, quirk, shirk, smirk, stirk, Turk,
work, yerk; frostwork, rework; Albu-
querque, handiwork, masterwork, overwork,
underwork.

-êrls: see -êarl.

-êrm, îrm: berm, derm, firm, germ, Herm,
perm, sperm, squirm, term, therm, worm;
affirm, confirm, glowworm, infirm, mis-
therm; disaffirm, isotherm. pachyderm.

-êrn: See -êarn.

-êrse: See -êrce.

-êrt, -îrt, ûrt: Bert, blurt, Burt, cert, chert,
curt, dirt, flirt, Gert, girt, gurt, hurt, pert,
"quirt", shirt, skirt, spirt, spurt, squirt,
syrt, vert, wert, Wirt, wort; advert, alert,
assert, avert, begirt, concert, convert, de-
sert, dessert, divert, engirt, exert, expert,
exsert, filbert, Gilbert, inert, insert, in-
vert, obvert, overt, pervert, revert, subvert,
transvert, ungirt, unhurt; Adelbert, con-
trovert, disconcert, Englebert, extrovert,
indesert, inexpert, intersert, introvert; ani-
madvert.

-êrth: See -êarth.

-êrve -ûrve: curve, nerve, sérve, swerve, verve; conserve, deserve, incurve, observe, outcurve, preserve, reserve, subserve, unnerve.

-es, -esce, -ess: Bess, bless, cess, chess, cress, dress, fess, guess, jess, Jess, Kress, less, mess, ness, press, stress, Tess, tress, yes; abscess, access, actress, address, aggress, assess, caress, compress, confess, depress, digress, distress, duress, egress, empress, excess, express, finesse, impress, ingress, largesse, Loch Ness, mattress, noblesse, obsess, oneness, oppress, possess, princess, profess, progress, recess, redress, regress, repress, sheerness, success, suppress, transgress, undress, unless; acquiesce, archeress, baroness, bottomless, coalesce, convalesce, dispossess, effervesce, hardiness, Inverness, obsolesce, opalesce, overdress, poetess, politesse, prophetess, repossess, shepherdess, sorceress, votaress, wilderness; nevertheless, proprietress. (Also many words with the suffix **-ness** as in "ugliness".)

-esh: flesh, fresh, mesh, nesh, thresh; afresh, enmesh, refresh, secesh.

-esk, -esque: desk, Esk; burlesque, Dantesque, grotesque, moresque; arabesque, barbaresque, chivalresque, gigantesque, picaresque, picturesque, Romanesque, sculpturesque, statuesque.

-est: best, blest, breast, Brest, cest, chest, crest, Gest, guest, hest, jest, lest, nest, pest, quest, rest, test, vest, west, wrest, zest; abreast, arrest, attest, behest, bequest, congest, contest, depressed, detest, devest, digest, distressed, divest, imprest, increst, ingest, inquest, invest, molest, obtest, protest, recessed, request, suggest, unblest, unguessed, unpressed; Alkahest, anapest, Bucharest, Budapest, Everest, interest, manifest, predigest, Trieste; disinterest. (See the preterites of many verbs in **-ess**, such as "stressed". Also a number of false rhymes in which the accent is not on the final syllable such as "conquest".)

-et, -ette: bet, Brett, Cette, debt, flet, fret, frett, get, jet, ket, let, Lett, met, net, pet, ret, set, sett, stet, sweat, threat, tret, vet, wet, yet; abet, aigrette, ailette, alette, backset, baguette, barbette, Barnett, beget, benet, beset, bewet, brevet, brunette, cadet, corvette, coquette, croquette, curvet, duet, forget, fossette, fourchette, fumette, gazette, genet, Gillette, inset, prisette, lunette, Nannette, offset, omelette, parquet, pipette, piquet, piquette, pirouette, quartette, quintet, regret, rosette, sestet, sextet, sunset, Thibet, Tibet, upset, vignette, wellmet; alphabet, amulet, anchoret, Antoinette, bassinet, bayonet, cabinet, calumet, casta-

41

net, cellaret, chansonette, cigarette, cover-
let, epaulet, epithet, etiquette, falconet,
farmerette, flannelette, floweret, globulet,
Juliet, laudaulet, lazarette, leaderette,
luncheonette, maisonette, marmoset, mar-
tinet, mignonette, minaret, minuet, novel-
ette, overset, parapet, parroket, pierette,
pirouette, quadruplet, sarcenet, serviette,
silhouette, somerset, statuette, suffragette,
tabaret, tourniquet, underset, wagonette.

-etch: etch, fetch, ketch, fletch, retch, sketch,
stretch. vetch, wretch; outstretch.

-ēte: See -ēat.

-eūd: See -ōōd.

-ēve: See -ēave.

-ew, -ieū, -ūe: blew, blue, boo, brew, chew,
crew, cue, dew, do, drew, due, ewe, few,
flew, flu, flue, glue, gnu, goo, grew, hew,
hue, Hugh, Jew, jue, knew, Lew, lieu, loo,
Lou, mew, moo, mu, new, nu, pew, queue,
rue, screw, shoe, shrew, skew, thew, threw,
through, to, too, true, two, view, who,
woo, yew, you, zoo; accrue, adieu, ado,
ague, anew, Anjou, askew, Baku, bamboo,
bedew, bellevue, beshrew, cachou, canoe,
cashew, cuckoo, curfew, curlew, debut, emu,
endue, ensue, eschew, Hindu, imbue, issue,
juju, menu, mildew, Peru, pooh-pooh, pur-
sue, purview, ragout, renew, review, sham-

poo, subdue, taboo, tattoo, tissue, undo, venue, voodoo, withdrew, yahoo, Zulu; avenue, barbecue, billet-doux, catechu, cockatoo, curlicue, interview, kangaroo, misconstrue, parvenu, rendezvous, residue, retinue, revenue, toodle-oo, Timbuktu, Kalamazoo, merci beaucoup. (Also see -ōō.)

-ex: cheques, Ex, flex, hex, lex, rex, Rex, sex, "specs", treks, vex; annex, apex, codex, complex, convex, index, perplex, reflex; circumflex. (The present tense of verbs and the plurals of nouns in -eck, as in "decks" and "wrecks".)

-ext: next, text; pretext. (Also -ex + ed as "vexed".)

-ey (ā): See -āy.

-ez: Fez, fez, sez, Les (for Leslie); Juarez, Suez; Marseillaise.

-ī: See -y.

-iar: (As in "liar", see two-syllable rhymes.)

-ib: bib, Bibb, crib, dib, drib, fib, gib, Gibb, glib, jib, nib, quib, rib, sib, squib; ad lib, Carib.

-ībe: bribe, gibe, jibe, kibe, scribe, tribe; ascribe, describe, imbibe, inscribe, prescribe, proscribe, subscribe, transcribe; circumscribe, diatribe, interscribe, superscribe.

-ic, -ick: brick, chic, chick, click, crick, dick,

Dick, flick, hick, kick, lick, mick, Mick,
nick, Nick, pick, prick, quick, rick, sic,
sick, slick, snick, spick, stick, thick, tic,
tick, trick, Vic, wick, Wick; beatnik, bes-
tick, caustic, heartsick, lovesick, sputnik,
toothpick, triptych, yardstick; acoustic, arsenic, artistic, bailiwick, Benedick, bishop-
ric, Bolshevik, candlestick, candlewick,
Catholic, chivalric, choleric, double-quick,
heretic, limerick, lunatic, maverick, politic,
rhetoric, single-stick, turmeric; arithmetic,
impolitic.

-ice, -ise (short): bice, Brice, dice, ice, gneiss,
lice, mice, nice, price, rice, slice, spice,
splice, thrice, trice, twice, vice, vise; ad-
vice, allspice, concise, device, entice, pre-
cise, suffice; paradise, sacrifice.

-ich: See **-itch.**

-ick: See **-ic.**

-ict: Pict, strict; addict, afflict, astrict, conflict, constrict, convict, delict, depict, edict,
evict, inflict, predict, relict, restrict; benedict, Benedict, contradict, derelict. (See
preterites of **-ick.**)

-id: bid, chid, Cid, did, fid, Gid, grid, hid,
kid, lid, mid, quid, rid, skid, slid, squid,
thrid, yid; amid, eyelid, forbid, Madrid,
outbid, outdid, unbid, undid; invalid, katy-
did, overbid, pyramid, underbid, unforbid.

-ide, -ied: bide, bride, chide, Clyde, glide, gride, guide, hide, Hyde, pied, pride, ride, Ryde, side, slide, snide, stride, tide, wide; abide, aside, astride, backside, backslide, beside, bedside, bestride, betide, broadside, bromide, Carbide, cockeyed, collide, confide, cowhide, cross-eyed, decide, deride, divide, elide, excide, hillside, inside, landslide, meek-eyed, misguide, noontide, outride, outside, outstride, pie-eyed, preside, provide, reside, seaside, subside, sulfide, wall-eyed, wayside, Yuletide; alongside, bonafide, coincide, countrified, dignified, eventide, fortified, fratricide, goggle-eyed, homicide, justified, matricide, misallied, override, parricide, patricide, peroxide, purified, qualified, regicide, riverside, satisfied, subdivide, suicide, unapplied, undertide, vitrified; formaldehyde, infanticide, insecticide, tyrannicide, vulpicide. (And "cried", "died", "signified", and about 70 other preterites of verbs in -y, -ie and -ye.)

-ides: ides; besides. (And add "s" to words in previous list.)

-idge: bridge, midge, ridge; abridge, cartridge, partridge; acreage, beverage, brokerage, cartilage, factorage, foliage, fuselage, hemorrhage, heritage, lineage, parentage, patronage, pilgrimage, privilege, sacrilege, tutelage, vicarage.

45

-idst: bidst, chidst, didst, hidst, midst, ridst, slidst; amidst, forbidst.

-ie: See -y.

-ief: See -ēef.

-iēge: liege, siege; besiege, prestige.

-iēnd: See -ēand.

-iēr: See -ēar.

-iēld: See -ēald.

-iērce: Bierce, fierce, Pearce, pierce, tierce; transpierce.

-iēve: See -ēave.

-if, -iff, -ẏph: biff, cliff, diff, glyph, griff, if, Jiff, miff, niff, quif, "Riff", skiff, sniff, stiff, tiff, whiff, wiff; handkerchief, hieroglyph, neckerchief, Teneriffe.

-ife: fife, Fife, knife, life, naif, rife, strife, wife; fishwife, goodwife, housewife, jackknife, midwife; afterlife.

-ift: clift, drift, gift, lift, rift, shift, shrift, sift, swift, thrift; adrift, snowdrift, spendthrift, spindrift, uplift. (Also preterites of verbs in -if.)

-ig: big, brig, dig, fig, gig, grig, jig, pig, prig, rig, shig, sprig, swig, trig, twig, Whig, wig; renege; guinea-pig, periwig, thimblerig, whirligig; thingumajig.

-igh: See -y.

-ight: See **-ite.**

-ign: See **-ine.**

-igue: See **-eague.**

-ike: bike, dyke, hike, Ike, like, Mike, pike, psych, shrike, spike, strike, type, Wyke; alike, dislike, Klondyke, manlike, midlike, mislike, turnpike, unlike, Vandyke; maidenlike, womanlike, workmanlike.

-il, -ill: bill, Bill, brill, chill, dill, drill, fill, frill, gill, grill, grille, hill, ill, jill, Jill, kill, mill, nil, pill, prill, quill, rill, shrill, skill, spill, squill, still, swill, thill, thrill, till, trill, twill, 'twill (it will), vill, will, Will; befrill, bestill, Brazil, distil, downhill, freewill, fulfil, instil, quadrille, Seville, until, unwill, uphill; chlorophyll, codicil, daffodil, domicile, imbecile, Louisville, versatile, volatile, whippoorwill.

-ilch: filch, milch, pilch, Zilch.

-ild: build, gild, guild; rebuild, unskilled; unfulfilled. (And preterites of -il words.)

-ild: aisled, child, Childe, mild, wild; beguiled, enfiled. (And preterites of verbs in -ile, as in "filed", "exiled".)

-ile, Isle, -yle: aisle, bile, chyle, file, guile, I'll, isle, Lyle, mile, Nile, pile, rile, smile, spile, stile, style, tile, vile, while, wile; Argyle, beguile, Carlyle, compile, defile,

47

exile, gentile, meanwhile, puerile, revile, servile, somewhile, tensile; Anglophile, crocodile, diastyle, domicile (verb), Francophile, infantile, juvenile, mercantile, peristyle, puerile, reconcile; bibliophile.

-ile (-ēl): See **-ēal.**

-ilk: bilk, ilk, milk, silk; spun silk.

-iln: biln, kiln, Milne.

-ilt: built, gilt, guilt, hilt, jilt, kilt, lilt, milt, quilt, silt, spilt, stilt, tilt, wilt; atilt, begilt, rebuilt, unbuilt, ungilt; Vanderbilt.

-ilth: filth, spilth, tilth.

-im: brim, dim, glim, grim, Grimm, gym, him, hymn, Jim, Kim, limb, limn, Lympne, prim, rim, shim, skim, slim, swim, Tim, trim, vim, whim; bedim, betrim, enlimn, pilgrim, prelim; antonym, cherubim, eponym, homonym, interim, pseudonym, Sanhedrim, seraphim, synonym.

-Ime: chime, chyme, climb, clime, crime, cyme, dime, grime, I'm, lime, Lyme, mime, prime, rhyme, rime, slime, thyme, time; bedtime, begrime, belime, berhyme, birdlime, daytime, lifetime, meantime, sublime, upclimb, Guggenheim, maritime, overtime, pantomime, paradigm, summertime, wintertime.

-Imes: betimes, sometimes. (Also **-Ime + s** as

48

in "chimes" and -yme + s as in "rhymes".)

-imp: blimp, "chimp", crimp, gimp, guimpe, imp, jimp, limp, pimp, primp, scimp, scrimp, shrimp, simp, skimp, tymp.

-impse: glimpse. (And pluralize words in above list.)

-in, -inn, -ine: been, bin, chin, din, djinn, fin, Finn, gin, Glynne, grin, in, inn, jinn, kin, lyn, Lynn, pin, quin, shin, sin, skin, spin, thin, tin, twin, whin, win; agrin, akin, bearskin, begin, Berlin, buckskin, chagrin, Corinne, herein, sidespin, tailspin, therein, unpin, wherein, within; alkaline, almandine, Argentine, aspirin, bulletin, Byzantine, cannikin, crinoline, crystalline, culverin, discipline, feminine, finickin, gelatin, genuine, glycerine, harlequin, heroine, Jacobin, javelin, jessamine, kilderkin, libertine, mandarin, mandolin, manikin, masculine, minikin, moccasin, origin, paladin, pavonine, peregrine, Philistine, ravelin, saccharine, sibylline, violin, zeppelin.

-inc: See -ink.

-ince: blintz, chintz, mince, prince, quince, rinse, since, Vince, wince; convince, evince, unprince. (Also, -int + s as in "hints".)

-inch: cinch, chinch, clinch, finch, flinch, inch, linch, lynch, pinch, winch; bepinch, Goldfinch, unclinch.

49

-inct, -inked: tinct; distinct, extinct, instinct, precinct, succinct; indistinct. (And preterites of verbs in **-ink,** as in "blinked".)

-ind and -ined: bind, blind, find, grind, hind, kind, mind, rind, wind; behind, inbind, mankind, purblind, remind, snow-blind, unbind, unkind, unwind; color-blind, disinclined, gavelkind, humankind, mastermind, undersigned, undesigned, unrefined, womankind. (And preterites of **-ign** and **-ine** words.)

-ind, -inned: ind, Scinde, wind; abscind, rescind; Rosalind, tamarind. (And preterites of verbs in **-in** and **-ine,** as in "pinned", and "disciplined".)

-ine: abine, brine, chine, dine, eyne, fine, kine, Klein, line, mine, nine, pine, Rhine, shine, shrine, sign, sine, spine, spline, Stein, swine, syne, thine, tine, trine, twine, tyne, vine, whine, wine; airline, align, assign, benign, beshine, calcine, canine, carbine, carmine, coastline, combine, condign, confine, consign, decline, define, design, divine, enshrine, entwine, feline, Holstein, incline, indign, lifeline, malign, moonshine, opine, outline, outshine, recline, refine, reline, repine, resign, saline, sunshine, supine, untwine, vulpine, woodbine; alkaline, anodyne, aquiline, Argentine, asinine, brigantine, Byzantine, celandine, Clementine, columbine, concubine, countermine, crystalline, disincline,

50

eglantine, incardine, interline, intertwine, iodine, leonine, palatine, porcupine, saturnine, serpentine, superfine, turpentine, underline, undermine, valentine, verperine.

-ine (ēne): See -ēan.

-ing: bing, bring, cling, ding, fling, king, ling, Ming, ping, ring, sing, sling, spring, sting, string, swing, synge, thing, thring, wing, wring, ying; evening, hireling, lifespring, mainspring, something, starveling, unsling, unstring; anything, chitterling, easterling, everything, underling, wedding-ring. (And more than 1,000 false rhymes in present participles, as in "happening", "issuing", etc.)

-inge: binge, cringe, fringe, hinge, Inge, singe, springe, stinge, tinge, twinge; astringe, befringe, impinge, infringe, syringe, unhinge.

-ink: blink, brink, chink, cinque, clink, drink, fink, gink, inc., jink, kink, link, mink, pink, prink, rink, shrink, sink, skink, slink, stink, swink, think, tink, trink, twink, wink, zinc; bethink; hoodwink, methink; bobolink, counter-sink, Humperdinck, interlink, tiddlywink.

-inks: See -inx.

-inse: See -ince.

-int: dint, flint, Flint, glint, hint, lint, mint, print, quint, splint, sprint, squint, stint, tint, vint; asquint, footprint, imprint, misprint, reprint, spearmint; peppermint.

-int: pint; ahint, behint.

-inth: plinth; absinthe, Corinth; hyacinth, labyrinth, terebinth.

-inx, -inks: jinx, lynx, minx, sphinx; larynx, methinks, salpinx, tiddlywinks. (And add "s" to nouns and verbs in -ink.)

-ip: blip, chip, clip, dip, drip, flip, grip, grippe, gyp, hip, kip, lip, nip, pip, quip, rip, scrip, ship, sip, skip, slip, snip, strip, tip, trip, whip, yip, zip, atrip, cowslip, equip, horsewhip, landslip, outstrip, transship, unship, unzip, warship. And false rhymes as follows: apprenticeship, battleship, censorship, championship, citizenship, chaplainship, deaconship, dictatorship, fellowship, guardianship, horsemanship, ladyship, partnership, penmanship, scholarship, sizarship, stewardship, workmanship and, etc.

-ipe: gripe, pipe, ripe, snipe, stipe, stripe, swipe, tripe, type, wipe; bagpipe, blowpipe, hornpipe, pitchpipe, sideswipe, tintype, unripe, windpipe; antitype, archetype, autotype, guttersnipe, linotype, monotype, overripe, prototype; daguerreotype, electrotype, stereotype.

-ipt: script; manuscript. (And preterites of verb s in -ip, as in "snipped".)

-ipse, -ips: eclipse, ellipse; apocalypse. (And add "s" to nouns and verbs in **-ip,** as in "snips".)

-ique: See **-ēak** and **-īc.**

-ir: See **-êr.**

-irch: See **-êarch.**

-ird: See **-êard.**

-ire, -yre: byre, choir, dire, fire, gyre, hire, ire, lyre, mire, pyre, quire, shire, sire, spire, squire, tire, tyre, Tyre, vire, wire; acquire, admire, afire, aspire, attire, bonfire, conspire, desire, empire, enquire, entire, esquire, expire, grandsire, inquire, inspire, perspire, quagmire, require, respire, retire, sapphire, satire, spitfire, suspire, transpire, wildfire. (See **iå** in list of two syllable rhymes.)

-irge: See **-êrge.**

-irk: See **-êrk.**

-irl: See **-êarl.**

-irm: See **-êrm.**

-irn: See **-êarn.**

-irp, -ûrp: burp, chirp, twerp; extirp, usurp, (Past tense to rhyme with "excerpt".)

-irst, -êrst, -ûrst: burst, curst, durst, erst, first, Hearst, Hurst, thirst, verst, worst; accurst, athirst, becurst, outburst, uncursed, unversed. (And preterites of verbs in **-êrce,**

53

-êrse, and -ûrse, as in "coerced", "versed" and "cursed".)

-îrt: See -êrt.

-îrth: See -êarth.

-is, -iss, -ice: bis, bliss, Chris, Diss, hiss, kiss, Liss, mis, Swiss, this, wys; abyss, amiss, dismiss, jaundice, remiss; armistice, artifice, avarice, Beatrice, benefice, chrysalis, cicatrice, coclatrice, cowardice, dentifrice, edifice, emphasis, genesis, nemesis, orifice, precipice, prejudice, prolapsis, synthesis, verdigris; analysis, antithesis, diaeresis, diathesis, hypostasis, hypothesis, liquorice, metatasis, metropolis, necropolis, paralysis, parenthesis; metamorphosis.

-is (iz), -iz: biz, fizz, friz, his, is, Liz, phiz, quiz, 'tis, viz, whiz, wiz; Cadiz.

-īse, -īze: guise, prise, prize, rise, size, wise; advise, apprise, arise, assize, baptize, capsize, chastise, cognize, comprise, demise, despise, devise, disguise, emprize, excise, incise, Judaize, misprize, moonrise, realize, remise, reprise, revise, sunrise, surmise, surprise, unwise, uprise; adonize, advertise, aggrandize, agonize, alkalize, analyze, appetize, atomize, authorize, barbarize, botanize, brutalize, canonize, cauterize, centralize, christianize, circumcise, civilize, climatize, colonize, compromise, criticize, crystallize, dogmatize, dramatize, ecstasize, emphasize, energize, enterprise, equalize, eulogize, exercise, exorcise, fertilize, feudalize, focalize, formalize, fossilize, fraternize, galvanize, gentilize, gormandize, Hellenize, humanize, hypnotize, idealize, idolize, improvise, jeopardize, journalize, legalize, lionize, localize, magnetize, martyrize, mechanize, memorize, mercerize, methodize, minimize, mobilize, modernize, moralize, nasalize, neutralize, organize, ostracize, otherwise, oxidize, paralyze, patronize, pauperize, penalize, pilgrimize, plagiarize, pluralize, polarize, pulverize, rapturize, recognize, rhapsodize, royalize, ruralize, sacrifice, satirize, scandalize, scrutinize, sermonize, socialize, specialize, subsidize, summarize, supervise, syllogize, sympathize, symphonize, synchronize, synthetize, tantalize, terrorize, tranquillize, tyrannize, vocalize, vulcanize, vulgarize ; acclimatize, actualize, allegorize, alphabetize, amalgamize, anatomize, antagonize, apologize, apostatize, apostrophize, astrologize, astronomize, authorize, capitalize, catholicize, characterize, circularize, commercialize, congenialize, contrariwise, decentralize, dehumanize, demobilize, democratize, demonetize, demoralize, deodorize, devitalize, dichotomize, disorganize, economize, epilo-

gize, epitomize, extemporize, externalize,
familiarize, fanaticize, federalize, hypothe-
size, imperialize, italicize, legitimize, liber-
alize, macadamize, materialize, mediatize,
militarize, mineralize, monopolize, national-
ize, naturalize, philosophize, phlebotomise,
popularize, puritanize, regularize, reor-
ganize, ritualize, secularize, sensualize, so-
liloquize, systematize, theologize, theoso-
phize, ventriloquize, visualize; American-
ize, anathematize, departmentalize, ethe-
ralize, etymologize, familiarize, materialize,
particularize, professionalize, proverbialize,
revolutionize, spiritualize, universalize; in-
stitutionalize, internationalize. (Also add
"s" to words ending in -y.)

-ish: dish, fish, Gish, knish, Nish, pish, squish,
tish, wish; anguish, bluefish, goldfish; gibberish, babyish, betterish, cleverish, devilish,
feverish, gibberish, heathenish, kittenish,
lickerish, quakerish, vaporish, waterish,
willowish, womanish, yellowish; impoverish.

-isk: bisk, bisque, brisk, disc, disk, frisk, risk,
whisk; asterisk, basilisk, obelisk, odalisque,
tamarisk.

-ism: chrism, ism, prism, schism: abysm, Baal-
ism, Babism, baptism, Buddhahism, deism,
Fascism, monism, purism, realism, snob-
bism, sophism, technism, theism, truism;

actinism, agonism, altruism, anarchism, aneurism, anglicism, animism, aphorism, archaism, asteism, atheism, atomism, babysim, barbarism, biblicism, bloomerism, bogeyism, Bolshevism, braggardism, brutalism, cabalism, Calvanism, cataclysm, catechism, centralism, Chauvinism, classicism, communism, cretinism, Darwinism, despotism, devilism, dualism, egotism, embolism, etherism, euphuism, exorcism, fairyism, fatalism, fetishism, feudalism, fossilism, frivolism, Gallicism, galvanism, heathenism, hedonism, heroism, hibernism, Hinduism, Hitlerism, humanism, hypnotism, idealism, Islamism, jockeyism, journalism, Judaism, laconism, Latinism, localism, loyalism, lyricism, magnetism, mannerism, mechanism, mesmerism, methodism, modernism, monkeyism, moralism, mysticism, nativism, nepotism, nihilism, occultism, optimism, organism, ostracism, pacifism, paganism, pantheism, paroxysm, pauperism, pedantism, pelmanism, pessimism, plagiarism, pugilism, pythonism, quietism, rabbinism, rheumatism, rigorism, royalism, ruralism, satanism, savagism, Saxonism, scepticism, socialism, solescism, stoicism, subtilism, syllogism, symbolism, synchronism, terrorism, tigerism, tribalism, vandalism, vocalism, verbalism, vulgarism, witticism, yankeeism, Zionism; absolutism, academism; achromatism, aestheticism, agnosticism, alcoholism, alienism, anachronism, anatomism, Anglicanism, animalism, antagonism, asceticism, capitalism, characterism, classicalism, clericalism, conservatism, democratism, determinism, diabolism, diplomatism, eclecticism, empiricism, evangelism, exoticism, expressionism, externalism, fanaticism, favoritism, federalism, generalism, histrionism, hyperbolism, idiotism, imperialism, impressionism, Italicism, Jesuitism, laconicism, liberalism, literalism, monasticism, naturalism, nominalism, parallelism, parasitism, paternalism, patriotism, pedagogism, philosophism, secularism, sensualism, separatism, subjectivism, sychophantism, universalism, ventriloquism; abolitionism, agrarianism, Americanism, colloquialism, colonialism, conventionalism, equestrianism, evolutionism, existentialism, histrionicism, imperialism, indeterminism, indifferentism, industrialism, materialism, medievalism, Orientalism, phalansterism, phenomenalism, professionalism, proverbalism, Republicanism, Utopianism, vernacularism, antiquarianism, bacchanalianism, Congregationalism, constitutionalism, cosmopolitanism, experimentalism, internationalism, presbyterianism, proletarianism, supernaturalism, Unitarianism, vegetarianism; humanitarianism, utilitarianism.

-iss: See **-is.**

-ist, -issed, -ẏst: cist, cyst, fist, gist, grist, hist, list, mist, schist, tryst, twist, whist, wist, wrist; artist, assist, Babist, baptist, blacklist, Buddhist, chartist, chemist, consist, Cubist, cyclist, deist, dentist, desist, dismissed, druggist, dualist, duellist, enlist, entwist, faddist, Fascist, florist, flutist, harpist, hymnist, insist, jurist, linguist, palmist, persist, psalmist, purist, realist, resist, simplist, sophist, statist, stylist, subsist, theist; alchemist, amethyst, amorist, atheist, beneficed, bicyclist, bigamist, bolshevist, Calvinist, casuist, catechist, coexist, colonist, colorist, columnist, communist, conformist, copyist, cymbalist, Darwinist, diarist, dogmatist, dramatist, dualist, egoist, eucharist, eulogist, extremist, fabulist, fatalist, fetishist, feudalist, fictionist, guitarist, Hebraist, hedonist, hellenist, herbralist, hobbyist, humanist, humorist, hypnotist, idealist, idolist, journalist, lapidist, latinist, loyalist, medallist, Methodist, modernist, moralist, motorist, novelist, oculist, optimist, organist, pacifist, passionist, pessimist, physicist, pianist, pietist, plagiarist, platonist, pluralist, pragmatist, publicist, pugilist, quietist, rapturist, rigorist, royalist, ruralist, satanist, satirist, scientist, scripturist, socialist, soloist, spe-

59

cialist, strategist, suffragist, symbolist, sympathist, synthesist, technicist, terrorist, theorist, unionist, verbalist, visionist, vitalist, vocalist, votarist; absolutist, academist, allegorist, analogist, anatomist, annualist, antagonist, apologist, athetist, biblicist, biologist, capitalist, chiropodist, classicalist, contortionist, corruptionist, cremationist, destructionist, devotionist, diplomatist, empiricist, enamelist, epitomist, eternalist, evangelist, externalist, federalist, fossilogist, illusionist, immortalist, liberalist, misogamist, monogamist, monopolist, mythologist, nationalist, naturalist, nominalist, obstructionist, opinionist, pathologist, perfectionist, philanthropist, philologist, progressionist, protagonist, protectionist, psychologist, rationalist, religionist, revivalist, ritualist, secularist, sensualist, sexualist, spiritualist, subjectivist, synonymist, technologist, telegraphist, telephonist, textualist, topographist, traditionist, ventriloquist, vocabulist, zoologist, anthropologist, archaeologist, bibliophilist, conversationist, educationalist, entomologist, epigrammatist, evolutionist, genealogist, horticulturist, instrumentalist, materialist, memorialist, mineralogist, occidentalist, oppositionist, Orientalist, ornithologist, pharmacologist, physiognomist, physiologist, preferentialist, prohibition-

ist, revolutionist, sensationalist, sentimen-
talist, transcendentalist, universalist; consti-
tutionalist, contraversialist, conversational-
ist, educationalist, experimentalist, individ-
ualist, institutionalist, intellectualist, mete-
orologist, ministerialist, supernaturalist.
(And preterites of verbs in -iss, as in
"kissed".)

-it, -ite: bit, bitt, chit, cit, fit, flit. frit, grit,
it, it, kit, knit, lit, mitt, nit, pit, Pitt, quit,
sit, skit, slit, smit, spit, split, sprit, tit, twit,
whit, wit, Witt, writ; acquit, admit, befit,
beknit, bowsprit, commit, demit, DeWitt,
emit, immit, misfit, moon-lit, omit, outfit,
outsit, outwit, permit, pewit, refit, remit,
respite, starlit, submit, sunlit, titbit, tomtit,
transmit, unfit, unknit, apposite, benefit,
counterfeit, definite, exquisite, favorite,
hypocrite, infinite, interknit, opposite, pre-
termit, preterite, recommit, requisite.

-itch: bitch, ditch, fitch, flitch, hitch, itch, lych,
niche, pitch, rich, snitch, stitch, switch,
twitch, which, witch; bewitch, distich, en-
rich, hemstitch, sandwich, unhitch.

-īte, -ight, -eīght: bight, bite, blight, bright,
cite, dight, Dwight, fight, flight, fright,
height, hight, kite, knight, light, might,
mite, night, pight, plight, quite, right, rite,
sight, site, sleight, slight, smite, spite,
sprite, tight, trite, white, wight, wright,

61

write; accite, affright, alight, aright, Baalite, bedight, benight, contrite, daylight, delight, despite, disunite, downright, eremite, excite, foresight, forthright, goodnight, ignite, incite, indite, insight, invite, midnight, moonlight, outright, polite, recite, requite, starlight, sunlight, tonight, twilight, unite, unsight, unwrite, zincite, zoolite; acolyte, aconite, anchorite, appetite, bedlamite, belemnite, bipartite, Canaanite, candlelight, Carmelite, chrysolite, composite, copyright, crystallite, disunite, dynamite, ebonite, erudite, expedite, Fahrenheit, grapholite, impolite, Israelite, Jacobite, midshipmite, Muscovite, neophyte, overnight, oversight, parasite, plebiscite, proselite, recondite, reunite, satellite, stalactite, stalagmite, Sybarite, troglodyte, underwrite, vulcanite, watertight, weathertight; cosmopolite, electrolyte, entomolite, meteorite, theodolite.

-ite: See -it.

-ith, -ẏth: fifth, frith, kith, myth, pith, sith, smith, with, withe; forthwith, herewith, Penrith, therewith, wherewith, zenith; acrolith, Arrowsmith, monolith; paleolith.

-īthe: blithe, hithe, Hythe, lithe, scythe, tithe, withe, writhe.

-its, -itz: Blitz, Fritz, quits, Ritz, Schlitz. (And plurals of words in -it.)

-ive: chive, Clive, dive, drive, five, gyve, hive, I've, live, rive, shive, shrive, skive, stive, strive, thrive, wive; alive, arrive, beehive, connive, contrive, deprive, derive, revive, survive, unhive; power drive.

-ive: give, live, sieve, spiv; active, captive, costive, cursive, forgive, furtive, massive, missive, motive, native, outlive, passive, pensive, relive, restive, sportive, votive; ablative, abductive, acquisive, amative, causative, combative, curative, curvative, expletive, formative, fugitive, genitive, lambative, laudative, laxative, lenitive, lucrative, narrative, negative, nutritive, primitive, pulsative, punitive, putative, quantitive, sanative, sedative, semblative, sensitive, siccative, substantive, talkative, tentative, transitive, vibrative, vocative; abdicative, accusative, affirmative, alternative, appelative, applicative, cogitative, comparative, consecutive, conservative, contemplative, contributive, copulative, correlative, declarative, decorative, definitive, demonstrative, derivative, derogative, desiccative, diminutive, distributive, emanative, executive, explicative, figurative, generative, illustrative, imperative, imputative, incarnative, indicative, infinitive, informative, inquisitive, insensitive, intuitive, justifactive, meditative, operative, palliative, performative, prepara-

63

tive, prerogative, preservative, prohibitive, precreative, provocative, recitative, reformative, reparative, restorative, retributive, speculative, superlative; accumulative, administrative, alliterative, appreciative, argumentative, authoritative, commemorative, communicative, co-operative, corroborative, defenerative, deliberative, depreciative, determinative, discriminative, eradicative, illuminative, imaginative, insinuative, interrogative, opinionative, prejuducative, recriminative, refrigerative, regenerative, remunerative, representative, reverberative, significative.

-ix: fix, mix, pyx, six, Styx; admix, affix, commix, infix, matrix, onyx, prefix, prolix, suffix, transfix, unfix; cicatrix, crucifix, fiddlesticks, intermix, politics, sardonyx, executrix. (And plurals of nouns in **-ick**, as in "kicks".)

-ō, -ōw, -eau, -ōe: beau, blow, bo, bow, co. (company), crow, do (music), doe, dough, eau, Flo, floe, flow, foe, fro, glow, go, grow, ho, hoe, Joe, know, lo, low, mot, mow, no, O, oh, owe, Po, pro, rho, roe, row, sew, show, sloe, slow, snow, so, sow, stow, strow, though, throe, throw, toe, tow, trow, whoa, woe, zoe; aglow, ago, although, banjo, below, bestow, Bordeaux, bravo, bureau, chapeau, chateau, cocoa, dado, de trop, depot, dido, duo, forego, foreknow, foreshow, heigh-ho, hello, how-so, inflow, jabot, long-bow, morceau, oboe, outflow, outgrow, pierrot, plateau, rainbow, rondeau, rouleau, Soho, tableau, trousseau, unknow, upgrow, upthrow, allegro, apropos, buffalo, bungalow, calico, cameo, comme-il faut, Diderot, domino, embryo, entrepot, Eskimo, gigolo, haricot, Idaho, indigo, momento, mistletoe, mulatto, nuncio, oleo, overflow, overgrow, overthrow, Pimlico, portico, proximo, stiletto, studio, tobacco, torpedo, tremolo, ultimo, undergo, under-tow, vertigo, volcano, Westward-ho; adagio, bravissimo, embroglio, fortissimo, incognito, intaglio, Ontario, pistachio; braggadacio, oratorio.

-ōach: broach, brooch, coach, loach, poach, roach; abroach, approach, cockroach, encroach, reproach.

-ōad, -ōde, -ōwed: bode, clode, code, goad, load, lode, mode, node, ode, road, rode, spode, strode, toad, woad; abode, bestrode, commode, corrode, erode, explode, forebode, unload; antipode, discommode, episode, incommode, lycopode, overload, pigeon-toed, unbestowed. (And preterites of verbs in **-ōe, -ōw** and **-ōwe.**)

-ōaf: goaf, loaf, oaf.

-ōak, -ōke: bloke, broke, choke, cloak, coak,

coke, croak, folk, joke, loke, moke, oak,
poke, sloke, smoke, soak, spoke, stoke,
stroke, toke, toque, woke, yoke, yolk; asoak,
awoke, baroque, bespoke, convoke, evoke,
forspoke, invoke, outbroke, provoke, revoke,
uncloak, unyoke; artichocke, counterstroke,
equiwoke, gentlefolk, masterstroke, under-
stroke.

-ōal, -ōle, -ōl, -ōll, -ōul, -ōwl: bole, boll, bowl,
coal, cole, dhole, dole, droll, foal, goal, hole,
jole, jowl, knoll, kohl, mole, pole, poll,
role, roll, scroll, shoal, shole, sole, soul, stole,
stroll, thole, toll, troll, vole, whole; cajole,
comptrol, condole, console, control, Creole,
enroll, extoll, inscroll, loophole, maypole,
parole, patrol, pistole, porthole, segol, tad-
pole, tophole, unroll, unsoul, uproll, virole;
aureole, banderole, barcarolle, buttonhole
camisole, capriole, caracole, casserole, cur-
tainpole, girasole, pigeon-hole, rigmarole,
self-control, Seminole, vacuole.

-ōam, -ōme: chrome, clomb, comb, dome, foam,
Frome, gnome, holm, home, loam, "mome"
(Carroll), Nome, ohm, pome, roam, Rome,
sloam, tome; afoam, befoam, endome,
Jerome, sea-foam; aerodrome, catacomb,
chromosome, currycomb, gastronome, hip-
podrome, metronome, microsome, mono-
chrome, palindrome, polychrome.

-ōan, ōne, -ōwn: blown, bone, cone, crone,

drone, flown, groan, grown, hone, Joan,
known, loan, lone, moan, mown, own,
phone, pone, prone, Rhone, roan, scone,
sewn, shown, Sloane, sown, stone, strown,
tone, throne, thrown, zone; alone, atone,
begroan, bemoan, bestrown, brimstone,
Cologne, condone, depone, dethrone, dis-
own, dispone, enthrone, engone, flagstone,
foreknown, foreshown, full-blown, grind-
stone, hailstone, intone, keystone, limestone,
milestone, moonstone, ozone, postpone, pro-
pone, trombone, unblown, ungrown, un-
known, unsewn, unsown; chaperone, corner-
stone, dictaphone, gramaphone, interpone,
knucklebone, megaphone, microphone, mon-
otone, overgrown, overthrown, saxophone,
semitone, telephone, unbeknown, undertone,
vitaphone, xylophone.

-ôar, -ôre: boar, Boer, bore, chore, core, corps,
door, floor, fore, frore, four, gore, hoar, lore,
more, nore, Nore, oar, o'er, pore, pour, roar,
score, shore, snore, soar, sore, store, swore,
tore, war, whore, wore, yore; adore, afore,
ashore, before, Cawnpore, claymore, deplore,
encore, explore, folklore, footsore, forbore,
foreshore, forswore, galore, heartsore, ig-
nore, implore, restore; albacore, battledore,
Baltimore, commodore, evermore, further-
more, heretofore, matador, nevermore, pina-
fore, sagamore, semaphore, Singapore,

sophomore, stevedore, sycamore, underscore.
(See ôr and ôor.)

-ôarse: See ôrse.

-ōast, -ōst: boast, coast, ghost, grossed, host,
most, oast, post, roast, toast; almost, en-
grossed, foremost, hindmost, riposte, sea-
coast, signpost; aftermost, bettermost,
furthermost, hindermost, hithermost, inner-
most, lowermost, nethermost, outermost,
undermost, uppermost, uttermost, western-
most.

-ōat, -ōte: bloat, boat, bote, Chote, coat, cote,
Croate, dote, float, gloat, goat, groat, moat,
mote, note, oat, quote, rote, shoat, smote,
stoat, throat, tote, vote, wrote; afloat, capote,
connote, demote, denote, devote, emote, foot-
note, lifeboat, misquote, outvote, promote,
remote, steamboat, topcoat, unquote; anec-
dote, antidote, assymptote, billygoat, creo-
sote, nanny goat, overcoat, petticoat, reding-
gote,, table d'hôte, underwrote; Witenage-
mot.

-ōath, -ōth: both, growth, loath, oath, quoth,
sloth, troth, wroth; Arbroath, betroth; after-
growth, overgrowth, undergrowth.

-ōathe: clothe, loathe; betrothe.

-ōax: coax, hoax. (And pluralize -ōak, -ōke,
as in "oaks", "jokes".)

-ob, -äb: blob, bob, Bob, cob, Cobb, dod, fob, glob, gob, hob, job, knob, lob, mob, nob, quab, rob, slob, snob, sob, squab, swab, throb; athrob, cabob, corncob, demob, hobnob, nabob; thingumbob.

-ōbe: globe, Job, lobe, Loeb, probe, robe; conglobe, disrobe, enrobe, unrobe; Anglophobe, Francophobe, Gallophobe, Slavophobe.

-ock: Bach, Bloch. block, bock, brock, chock, clock, cock, crock, doc, dock, flock, frock, hock, jock, Jock, knock, Knoche, loch, lock, Mach, mock, pock, roc, rock, shock, smock, sock, stock; acock, amok, Bangkok, bedrock, belock, bemock, deadlock, fetlock, Hancock, hemlock, padlock, peacock, petcock, shamrock, Sherlock, Shylock, tick-tock, unfrock, unlock, woodcock; alpenstock, Antioch, billycock, havelock, hollyhock, interlock, Little Rock, shuttlecock, weathercock.

-oct: concoct, decoct, shell-shocked. (And preterites of **-ock,** as in "locked".)

-od: clod, cod, God, hod, nod, odd, plod, pod, prod, quad, quod, rod, scrod, shod, sod, squad, tod, trod, wad; ballade, façade, roughshod, roulade, slipshod, unshod, untrod; demi-god, golden-rod, lycopod, platypod, promenade.

-odge: bodge, dodge, hodge, lodge, podge, splodge, stodge; dislodge, hodge-podge.

-ōe: See -ō.

-ôff: cough, doff, koff, off, prof, scoff, shroff, "soph", toff, trough; takeoff; philosophe.

-ôft: croft, loft, oft, soft, toft; aloft; undercroft. (And preterites of verbs in **-off**.)

-og, ogue: bog, clog, cog, flog, gog, grog, jog, nog, Prague, slog, shog, stog; agog, eggnogg, incog, unclog, demogogue, epilogue, monologue, pedagogue, synagogue.

-ôg, -ôgue: dog, fog, frog, hog, log, bulldog, analogue, apologue, catalogue, decalogue, dialogue, duologue, pettifog, travelogue.

-ōgue: brogue, rogue, vogue; prorogue; disembogue.

-oice: Boyce, choic, Joyce, voice; invoice, rejoice, Rolls-Royce.

-oid: Boyd, Floyd, Freud, Lloyd, void; avoid, devoid, Negroid, ovoid, rhomboid, tabloid; alkaloid, aneroid, anthropoid, asteroid, celluloid, Mongoloid, trapezoid; paraboloid, pyramidoid. (And preterites of verbs in **-oy**, as "destroyed".)

-oil: boil, Boyle, broil, coil, Doyle, foil, Hoyle, moil, oil, roil, soil, spoil, toil; despoil, embroil, entoil, gumboil, Lough Foyle, parboil, recoil, tinfoil, trefoil, turmoil, uncoil; counterfoil, disembroil, quatrefoil. (See **-oyàl**.)

-ōin, -ōyne: Boyne, coign, coin, foin, groin, groyne, join, loin, quoin; adjoin, benzoin, Burgoyne, conjoin, Des Moines, disjoin, enjoin, purloin, rejoin, sejoin, sirloin, subjoin; tenderloin.

-oint: joint, oint, point; adjoint, anoint, appoint, aroint, conjoint, disjoint, repoint, West Point; counterpoint, coverpoint, disappoint, reappoint.

-oise, -oys: froise, noise, poise, Troyes; counterpoise, equipoise, Illinois, Iroquois; avoirdupois. (And add "s" to -oy.)

-oist: foist, hoist, joist, moist, voiced; invoiced, rejoiced. (And add "s" to -oice.)

-oit: coit, doit, quoit; adroit, Beloit, dacoit, Detroit, exploit, introit; maladroit.

-ōke: See -ōak.

-ol, -oll: doll, loll, Moll, poll, Sol; atoll, extol; alcohol, capitol, folderol, parasol, vitriol.

-ōl, -ōll, -ōle: See -ōal.

-ōld: bold, cold, fold, gold, hold, mold, mould, old, scold, sold, told, wold; behold, blindfold, cuckold, enfold, foothold, foretold, freehold, household, retold, stronghold, threshold, toehold, twofold, unfold, untold, uphold, withhold; manifold, marigold, overbold. (And preterites of -ōal, -ōle, -ōll and -ōwl.)

-ōlk: See -ōak.

-ōlt: bolt, colt, dolt, holt, jolt, molt, poult, volt; revolt, unbolt; thunderbolt.

-olve: solve; absolve, convolve, devolve, dissolve, evolve, involve, resolve, revolve.

-om: bomb, dom, from, pom, "Prom", rhomb, Somme, Tom; aplomb, pogrom, pom-pom, therefrom, tom-tom, wherefrom.

-ōme: See -ōam.

-omp: comp, pomp, romp, stomp, swamp.

-ompt: prompt, romped, swamped.

-on: Bonn, con, don, John, non, swan, wan, yon; anon, Argonne, Aswan, bonbon, Canton, Ceylon, chiffon, cretonne, icon, neutron, proton, upon, Yvonne; amazon, autophon, Babylon, benison, celadon, dies non, gonfalon, hereupon, lexicon, marathon, narbonne, octagon, Oregon, paragon, Parthenon, pentagon, polygon, Rubicon, silicon, tarragon, thereupon, phenomenon. (See -un for some words of three syllables ending in -on as in "champion".)

-ôn: on, "scone" (Scotch), begon, bygone, hereon, undergone. (Also see -ăwn.)

-once, -onse: nonce, ponce, sconce, wants; ensconce, response, séance, liederkranz. (For rhymes to "once", see -unce.)

-ond, -onned: blond, blonde, bond, fond, frond,

72

pond, wand, yond; abscond, beyond, despond, diamond, respond; correspond, co-respond, demimonde, vagabond. (And preterites of verbs in **-on**, as in "conned".)

-ōne: See **-un**.

-ōne: See **-ōan**.

-ong: gong, prong, thong, throng, tong, ding-dong, diphthong, Hongkong, mahjongg, ping-pong.

-ong: long, song, strong, Tong, wrong, along, belong, dugong, headlong, headstrong, life-long, oblong, prolong; evensong, overlong.

-onk: bonk, conch, conk, honk, plonk. (For "Bronx", add "s" to above.)

-ont: font, want; Vermont; Hellespont.

-ōnt: don't, wont, won't.

-önt: front. See **-unt**.

-onze: bonze, bronze, "onze" (French.) (And add "s" to words in **-on**, as in "cons".)

-ōō: See **-ew**.

-ōod: See **-ud**.

-ood: could, good, hood, should, stood, wood, would; childhood, Goodwood, manhood, un-hood, wildwood, withstood; babyhood, broth-erhood, fatherhood, hardihood, Hollywood, likelihood, livelihood, maidenhood, mother-hood, neighborhood, Robin Hood, sandal-wood, sisterhood, understood, widowhood;

73

misunderstood.

-ōōd (as in "food"), **-ēud, -ewed, üde:** brood,
Bude, crude, dude, feud, food, Jude, lewd,
mood, nude, prude, rood, rude, shrewd,
snood, you'd, who'd; allude, collude, con-
clude, delude, denude, detrude, elude, étude,
exclude, extrude, exude, illude, include, in-
trude, obtrued, occlude, preclude, prelude,
protrude, secude; altitude, amplitude, as-
suetude, attitude, beatitude, certitude, con-
suetude, crassitude, desuetude, finitude, for-
titude, gratitude, habitude, interlude, lassi-
tude, latitude, longitude, magnitude, man-
suetude, multitude, parvitude, platitude,
plenitude, promptitude, pulchritude, quie-
tude, restitude, sanctitude, servitude, soli-
tude ; disquietude, exactitude, inaptitude,
incertitude, ineptitude, infinitude, ingrati-
tude, necessitude, serenitude, similitude,
solicitude. (See under **-ew** for preterites of
verbs in **-ew, -ō, -üe**.)

-ōōf: goof, hoof, oof, pouf, proof, roof, spoof,
woof; aloof, behoof, disproof, fireproof, rain-
proof, reproof, Tartuffe; waterproof, weath-
erproof.

-ook: book, brook, cook, crook, hook, look,
nook, rook, shook, spook, took; betook,
Chinook, forsook, mistook, nainsook, out-
look, partook; overlook, overtook, pocket-
book, undertook.

-ōōl, -ūle: buhl, cool, drool, fool, ghoul, Goole, pool, Poole, rule, school, spool, stool, tool, tulle, who'll, Yule; ampoule, befool, footstool, home rule, misrule, toadstool, sporrule, Stamboul, whirlpool; Istanbul, Liverpool, molecule, overrule, ridicule, vestibule. (See **-ūle**, with diphthong, as in "mule". See also, **-ūĕl** in two-syllable rhymes as in "fuel".)

-ool: wool. See **-ul.**

-ōōm, -ūme: bloom, boom, broom, brougham, brume, coomb, coombe, doom, flume, fume, gloom, groom, loom, plume, rheum, room, spoom, spume, tomb, whom, womb, zoom; abloom, assume, Batoum, beplume, bridegroom, consume, costume, entomb, exhume, Ezroum, Fiume, heirloom, Khartoum, legume, perfume, presume, relume, resume, simoon, subsume, unplume, untomb; anteroom, diningroom, disentomb, drawingroom, dressingroom, hecatomb, reassume. (See **-ūme** with diphthong, as in "fume".)

-ōōn, ūne: boon, Boone, coon, croon, Doon, dune, goon, hewn, June, loon, lune, Lune, moon, noon, prune, rune, screwn, shoon, soon, spoon, strewn, swoon, Troon, tune; attune, baboon, balloon, bassoon, bestrewn, buffoon, cartoon, cocoon, commune, doubloon, dragoon, Dunoon, eftsoon, eschewn, festoon, forenoon, galloon, harpoon, high noon, immune, impugn, jejune, lagoon, lampoon, maroon, midnoon, monsoon, oppugn, platoon, poltroon, pontoon, quadroon, raccoon, Rangoon, shalloon, simoon, spittoon, tycoon, typhoon, walloon; afternoon, brigadoon, honeymoon, importune, macaroon, musketoon, octoroon, opportune, pantaloon, picaroon, picayune, rigadoon. (See -ūne with diphthong, as in "tune".)

-ōōp, -oūp: coop, croup, droop, drupe, dupe, goop, group, hoop, jupe, Krupp, loop, poop, scoop, sloop, snoop, soup, stoop, stoup, stupe, swoop, troop, troupe, whoop; recoup, unhoop; Guadeloupe, nincompoop. (See -ūpe.)

-ōor: boor, floor, moor, more, poor, Ruhr, spoor, tour, you're; amour, contour, detour; blackamoor, paramour. (See -ūre, -ewer in two-syllable rhymes, and -ōar.)

-ōōse, -ūce, -ūice (when pronounced -ōōse, short): Bruce, deuce, goose, juice, loose, moose, noose, puce, sluice, spruce, truce, use, zeus; abduce, abstruse, abuse, adduce, burnoose, caboose, conduce, deduce, diffuse, disuse, excuse, induce, misuse, obtuse, papoose, produce, profuse, recluse, reduce, seduce, Toulouse, traduce, vamoose; introduce, reproduce; hypotenuse. (Also see -uce.)

-ōōse (long), -ōōze, -ūes: blues, booze, bruise,

choose, cruise, lose, Ouse, ooze, ruse, shoes, snooze, trews, whose, who's; enthuse, peruse. (Compare **-use**, as in "fuse", and see **-ew**,

-ieū, **-ue** and **-ōō** for plurals of nouns and third person singular of verbs, as in "pews", adieus, "hues", etc.)

-ōōst, -ūced, -ūsed (sharp); coost, juiced, loosed, noosed, roost, suiced, spruced, used; adduced, conduced, deduced, educed, induced, produced, reduced, seduced, subduced; superinduced.

-oot (short): foot, put, soot; afoot, forefoot; pussyfoot, underfoot.

-ōōt, -ūte: boot, bruit, brute, chute, coot, flute, fruit, hoot, jute, loot, moot, root, route, shoot, skoot, toot; adjute, Beirut, cahoot, Canute, cheroot, galloot, recruit, uproot; arrowroot, attribute, overshoot, parachute, waterchute. (See **-ūte** with diphthong, as in "cute", "newt", etc.)

-ōōth (short th) **-ūth:** booth, couth, ruth, Ruth, sleuth, sooth, "strewth", tooth, truth, youth; Duluth, forsooth, uncouth, untruth, vermouth.

-ōōth (length): smooth, soothe.

-ōōve: groove, hoove, move, prove, who've, you've; amove, approve, behoove, disprove, improve, remove, reprove; disapprove.

-ōōze: See -ōōse.

-op: bop, chop, cop, crop, drop, flop, fop, hop,
lop, mop, plop, pop, prop, shop, slop, sop,
stop, strop, swap, top, whop, wop; Aesop,
atop, bedrop, co-op, eavesdrop, estop, flip-
flop, foretop, galop, snowdrop, tiptop, un-
stop; ginger-pop, lollipop, overtop, soda
pop, underprop.

-öp: develop. See **-up.**

-ōpe, -ōap: cope, dope, grope, hope, lope,
mope, nope, ope, pope, rope, scope, slope,
soap, taupe, tope, trope; elope, Good Hope;
antelope, antipope, bioscope, cantaloupe,
envelope, gyroscope, horoscope, interlope,
isotope, microscope, misanthrope, periscope,
polyscope, stethoscope, telescope; helioscope,
heliotrope, kaleidoscope.

-opse, -ops: copse. (And extend **-op.**)

-opt: copped, copt, dropped; adopt, out-
cropped, uncropped, unstopped. (And preterites of verbs in **-op.**)

-ôr: for, lor, nor, or, Thor, tor, war; abhor,
lessor, señor, therefore, ancestor, corridor,
councillor, counsellor, cuspidor, dinosaur,
Ecuador, escritoire, Labrador, legator,
matador, metaphor, meteor, minotaur,
monitor, mortgagor, orator; picador, Sal-
vador, servitor, troubador, visitor, warrior; ambassador, apparitor, conspirator,

78

contributor, depositor, executor, expositor, inheritor, inquisitor, progenitor, proprietor, solicitor, superior, toreador, ulterior; primogenitor.

-ör: donor, furor, junior, senior, vendor; auditor, bachelor, chancellor, conqueror, creditor, editor, emperor, janitor, senator, warrior; ambassador, anterior, competitor, excelsior, exterior, inferior, interior, posterior.

-ôrce, -ôrse, -ôarse, -ôurce: coarse, corse, course, force, gorse, hoarse, horse, Morse, Norse, source, torse; concourse, discourse, divorce, endorse, enforce, perforce, recourse, remorse, resource, sea horse, unhorse; hobbyhorse, intercourse, reinforce, watercourse.

-ôrch: Borsch, porch, scorch, torch.

-ôrd (as in "cord"): See -ôard.

-örd (as in "word"): See -êard.

-ôrge: forge, George, gorge; disgorge, engorge, regorge; overgorge.

-ôrk: cork, Cork, fork, pork, stork, torque, York; New York, pitchfork, uncork.

-örld: world. See -earled.

-ôrm: form, norm, storm, swarm, warm; bestorm, conform, deform, Great Orme, inform, misform, perform, reform, transform,

79

unwarm, upswarm; aeriform, chloroform, cruciform, cuneiform, misinform, multiform, thunderstorm, uniform, vermiform; iodoform.

-ôrn, ôrne: born, borne, bourn, corn, horn, lorn, morn, mourn, scorn, shorn, sorn, shorn, sworn, thorn, torn, warn, worn; acorn, adorn, blackthorn, buckthorn, Cape Horn, first-born, foghorn, forborne, forewarn, forlorn, forsworn, greenhorn, Leghorn, lovelorn, outworn, popcorn, suborn, toilworn, unborn; barley-corn, Capricorn, disadorn, longicorn, peppercorn, readorn, unicorn. (See **-ôurn** and **-ăwn.**)

-ôrp: dorp, thorp, warp.

-ôrse: See **-ôrce.**

-ôrt: bort, court, fort, forte, mort, ort, port, porte, quart, short, snort, sort, sport, swart, thwart, tort, wart; abort, assort, athwart, cavort, cohort, comport, consort, contort, deport, disport, distort, escort, exhort, export, extort, import, passport, purport, rapport, report, resort, retort, seaport, support, transport; misreport.

-ôrth: forth, fourth, north, Porth, swarth; henceforth, thenceforth.

-ōse (short "s"): close, cose, dose, gross; engross, floccose, gibbose, globose, glucose, jocose, morose, nodose, verbose; cellulose, comatose, diagnose, foliose, grandiose, overdose, underdose ; Barbados.

-ōse (-ōze): chose, close, clothes, does (plural of "doe"), doze, froze, gloze, hose, nose, pose, prose, "pros", rose, Rose, those; Ambrose, arose, banjos, compose, depose, depots, disclose, dispose, enclose, expose, foreclose, impose, inclose, Montrose, oppose, repose, suppose, transpose, unclose, unfroze; decompose, discompose, indispose, interpose, predispose, presuppose, recompose, superpose, tuberose. (For more than 60 other good rhymes, see plurals of nouns and third person singulars of verbs in -ō, -ōw and -ōe.)

-ösh: See -äsh.

-ôss: boss, Cos, cross, doss, dross, floss, fosse, gloss, "Goss", hoss, joss, loss, moss, os, poss, Ross, sauce, toss; across, cerebos, enboss, lacrosse, reredos; albatross, applesauce.

-ôst: cost, frost, lost, wast; accost, exhaust; holocaust, pentecost. (And preterites of -ôss, as in "bossed".)

-ōst: See -ōast.

-ot, -otte: blot, clot, cot, dot, Dot, got, grot, hot, jot, knot, lot, mot, not, plot, pot, rot, scot, Scot, shot, slot, snot, sot, spot, squat, swat, swot, tot, trot, watt, what, wot,

81

yacht; allot, boycott, calotte, capot, cocotte, culotte, dogtrot, ergot, forgot, foxtrot, garotte, gavotte, kumquat, loquat, somewhat, unknot; Aldershot, aliquot, apricot, bergamot, camelot, chariot, counterplot, eschalot, gallipot, Hottentot, Huguenot, idiot, Lancelot, misbegot, patriot, polygot, unbegot, undershot; forget-me-not.

-otch: blotch, botch, crotch, notch, potch, scotch, Scotch, splotch, swatch, watch; hopscotch, hotchpotch, topnotch.

-ōte: See **-ōat.**

-ōth: See **-ōath.**

-ôth: broth, cloth, froth, Goth, moth, troth, wroth; betroth, broadcloth, sackcloth; Ashtaroth, behemoth, Ostrogoth, Visigoth.

-ouch: couch, crouch, grouch, ouch, pouch, slouch, vouch; avouch; scaramouch. (For "touch," see **-uch.**)

-ouch (soft **ch**): mouch; bedouch.

-oud, -owd: cloud, crowd, dowd, loud, proud, shroud, Stroud; aloud, becloud, beshroud, encloud, enshroud, unbowed, uncloud, unshroud; disendowed, overcloud, overcrowd, thundercloud. (And preterites of **-ow**, as in "bowed".)

-ough: See **-ō, -ock, -off, -ōw, -uf.**

-ôught: See **-ăught.**

82

-ōul: See -ōal.

-ōuld: See -ōld.

-ounce: bounce, flounce, frounce, ounce, pounce, trounce; announce, denounce, enounce, pronounce, renounce. (Also, the plurals of -ount, as in "counts".)

-ound, -owned: bound, found, ground, hound, mound, pound, round, sound, wound; abound, aground, around, astound, background, bloodhound, compound, confound, dumbfound, expound, hidebound, homebound, icebound, inbound, outbound, profound, propound, rebound, redound, renowned, resound, spellbound, surround, unbound, unfound, unsound; underground, merry-go-round. (And preterites and adjectives of words in -own, as in "clowned" and "renowned".)

-oūnd: See preterites of verbs in ōōn, as in "crooned".

-ounge: lounge, scrounge.

-ount: count, fount, mount; account, amount, discount, dismount, miscount, recount, remount, surmount; catamount, paramount, tantamount.

-oūp: See -ōōp.

-our: dour, flour, hour, our, scour, sour; bescour, besour, deflour, devour. See **-owėr** in

-ôurd: gourd, Lourdes, moored. (And preterites of -ôr, -ōre, -ōar words.)

-ôurn: bourn, mourn. (See -ôrn.)

-ôurse: See -ôrce.

-ous: See -us.

-ouse (short): blouse, douse, grouse, house,
louse, mouse, nous, souse, spouse, Strauss;
backhouse, doghouse, madhouse, outhouse,
penthouse, poorhouse, storehouse, ware-
house, workhouse; Fledermaus, flindermouse.

-ouse (-ouze): drowse, blouse, blowze,
browse, house (verb), rouse, touse;
carouse (verb), expouse, unhouse, up-
rouse. (And plurals of nouns and third
person singulars of verbs in -ow and
-ough, as in "brows", "bows", "boughs"
and "ploughs".)

-out: bout, clout, doubt, drought, flout, gout,
grout, knout, kraut, lout, nowt, out, owt,
pout, rout, scout, snout, spout, sprout,
stout, tout, trout; about, beshout, bespout,
devout, knockout, mahout, redoubt, thereout,
throughout, without; gadabout, hereabout,
knockabout, roundabout, sauerkraut, stir-
about, thereabout, whereabout.

-outh: drouth, Louth, mouth, south. (For
rhymes to "youth", see -ōōth.)

84

-ŏve: dove, glove, love, of, shove; above, be-
love, foxglove, hereof, thereof, unglove,
whereof; ladylove, turtledove.

-ōve: clove, cove, dove, drove, grove, hove,
Hove, Jove, mauve, rove, shrove, stove,
strove, throve, trove, wove; alcove, behove;
interwove, treasure-trove. **(-ove,** as in
"proove", **-ōōve.)**

-ow, -ough: bough, bow, brow, chow, cow,
dhow, frau, how, now, plough, plow,
prow, row, scow, slough, Slough, sow, tau,
thou, trow, wow, vow; allow, avow, bow-
wow, endow, enow, Foochow, highbrow,
kowtow, landau, lowbrow, Mau Mau, meow,
Moldau, Moscow, powwow, snowplow, some-
how; anyhow, disallow, disavow, disendow,
middlebrow.

-ōw: See **-ō.**

-ōwed: See **-ōde.**

-owl, -oul: cowl, foul, fowl, growl, howl,
jowl, owl, prowl, scowl, yowl; befoul, water-
fowl. (Compare **-owél** in two syllable
rhymes.)

-own: brown, clown, crown, down, drown,
frown, gown, noun, town; adown, decrown,
discrown, downtown, embrown, pronoun,
renown, uptown; eiderdown, hand-me-down,
tumble-down, upside down.

-ōwn: See **-ōan.**

-owned: See -ound.

-ōws: See -ōse.

-ox, -ocks: box, "chocs.", cox, fox, lox, ox, phlox, pox, sox, vox; approx, bandbox, hatbox, icebox, mailbox, postbox, smallpox; chickenpox, equinox, orthodox, paradox; heterodox. (And plurals of nouns and third person singulars of verbs in -ock.)

-oy: boy, buoy, cloy, coy, gloy, goy, hoy, joy, oy, ploy, poi, soy, toy, troy, Troy; ahoy, alloy, Amoy, annoy, convoy, decoy, deploy, destroy, employ, enjoy, envoy, hoi polloi, Leroy, Savoy, sepoy, yoi-yoi!, corduroy, Illinois, Iroquois, overjoy, pomeroy, saveloy.

-oys: See -oise.

-ōze: See -ōse.

-ub: bub, blub, chub, club, cub, drub, dub, grub, hub, nub, pub, rub, scrub, shrub, snub, stub, sub, tub; hubbub; sillabub, Beelzebub.

-ūbe: boob, cube, "rube", Rube, tube; jujube.

-ūce, -ūse: Bruce, duce, juice, puce, use, (noun); abstruse, abuse (noun), conduce, deduce, diffuse, educe, excuse (noun), obtuse, produce, reduce, refuse (noun), seduce; traduce, introduce. (See -ōōse, (hards), and under same heading.)

-uch, -utch: clutch, crutch, Dutch, hutch,

much, smutch, such, touch; retouch; inasmuch, insomuch, overmuch.

-uck: buck, chuck, cluck, duck, luck, muck, pluck, puck, Puck, ruck, shuck, struck, stuck, suck, truck, tuck; amok, amuck, awestruck, Canuck, ill-luck, misluck, pot-luck, roebuck, woodchuck, horrorstruck, terrorstruck, thunder-struck, wonderstruck.

-ucked: See -uct.

-ucks: See -ux.

-uct, -ucked: duct; abduct, conduct (verb), construct, deduct, induct, instruct, obstruct; aqueduct, misconduct, oviduct, usufruct, viaduct. (And preterites of verbs in **-uck,** as in "mucked".)

-ud: blood, bud, cud, dud, flood, mud, rudd, scud, spud, stud, sud, thud; bestud, lifeblood, rosebud.

-ūde: See -ōōd.

-udge: budge, drudge, fudge, grudge, judge, nudge, Rudge, sludge, smudge, snudge, trudge; adjudge, begrudge, forejudge, misjudge, prejudge, rejudge.

-ūe: See -ew.

-uff: bluff, buff, chough, chuff, clough, cuff, duff, fluff, Gough, gruff, guff, huff, luff, muff, puff, rough, ruff, scruff, scuff, slough, snuff, sough, stuff, tough, tuff; bepuff, besnuff, breadstuff, enough, rebuff; blind-man's-buff, counterbuff, powder-puff.

-uft: cruft, tuft; candytuft. (And past participles of verbs in **-uff**.)

-ūise: See **-ōōse**.

-ūit: See **-ōōt**.

-uīse: See **-īze**.

-ug: bug, chug, drug, dug, hug, jug, lug, mug, plug, pug, rug, shrug, slug, smug, snug, thug, tug, ugh; humbug; bunnyhug, doodlebug, jitterbug.

-ūke: duke, fluke, Juke, Luke, puke, snook, spook, uke; archduke, caoutchouc, peruke, rebuke; Heptateuch, Hexateuch, mameluke, Marmaduke, Pentateuch.

-ul, -ull (as in "bull"): bull, full, pull, wool; abull, annul, cupful, graceful, lambswool; beautiful, bountiful, dutiful, fanciful, masterful, merciful, pitiful, plentiful, powerful, sorrowful, teaspoonful, wonderful, worshipful; tablespoonful.

-ul, -ull (as in "dull"): cull, dull, gull, hull, Hull, lull, mull, null, scull, skull, trull; annul, bulbul, mogul, numskull, seagull; disannul.

-ūle: fuel, mewl, mule, pule, tuhl, you'll, Yule; ampule; molecule, reticule, ridicule, vestibule. (See **-ōōl**, and under same heading,

88

-ule, without "u" sound, as in "rule". Also
-ūēl in two-syllable rhymes.)

-ulge: bulge; divulge, effulge, indulge, pro-
mulge.

-ulk: bulk, hulk, pulque, skulk, sulk.

-ulp: gulp, pulp, sculp.

-ulse: mulse, pulse; appulse, convulse, ex-
pulse, impulse, insulse, repulse.

-ult: cult, ult; adult, consult, exult, insult, oc-
cult, result, tumult; catapult, difficult.

-um: Brum, bum, chum, come, crumb, drum,
dumb, from, glum, gum, hum, mum, numb,
plum, plumb, rum, scum, scrum, slum,
some, strum, stum, sum, swum, thrum,
thumb; become, benumb, humdrum, spec-
trum, succumb; burdensome, cardamom,
Christendom, cranium, cumbersome, dreari-
some, flunkeydom, frolicsome, heathendom,
humorsome, laudanum, martyrdom, maxi-
mum, meddlesome, minimum, misbecome,
nettlesome, odium, opium, overcome, pabu-
lum, pendulum, platinum, premium, quar-
relsome, quietsome, radium, rebeldom, spec-
ulum, tedium, troublesome, tweedledum,
tympanum, vacuum, venturesome, weari-
some, worrisome, wranglesome; adventure-
some, chrysanthemum, compendium, deliri-
ium, empirium, encomium, exordium, fee-fi-
fo-fum, geranium, gymnasium, harmonium,

89

magnesium, millenium, opprobrium, palladium, petroleum, residuum, sensorium, solatium, symposium; auditorium, crematorium, equilibrium, pandemonium, sanitarium.

-ūme: fume, plume, spume; assume, consume, exhume, Fiume, illume, perfume, presume, relume, resume; reassume. (Compare -ōōm.)

-ump: bump, chump, clump, crump, dump, frump, grump, gump, hump, jump, lump, mump, plump, pump, rump, slump, stump, sump, thump, trump, tump, ump; bethump, mugwump.

-un: bun, done, dun, fun, gun, Hun, none, nun, one, pun, run, shun, son, spun, stun, sun, ton, tun, won; begun, foredone, forerun, homespun, outdone, outrun, rerun, someone, undone, unrun; Albion, amazon, benison, cinnamon, colophon, Chesterton, galleon, ganglion, garrison, gonfalon, jettison, octagon, orison, overdone, paragon, pentagon, polygon, simpleton, singleton, skeleton, unison, venison ; accordion, companion, oblivion, phenomenon.

-unce: bunce, dunce, once. (Also, see -unt + s, as in "hunts".)

-unch: brunch, bunch, Clunch, crunch, hunch, lunch, munch, punch, scrunch.

-unct, -unked: bunked, flunked; adjunct, defunct, debunked.

-und: bund, fund; fecund, jocund, obtund, refund, rotund; cummerbund, moribund, obrotund, rubicund, verecund. (And preterites of verbs in -un, as in "punned".)

-ūne: dune, hewn, June, tune, viewn; commune, immune, impugn, jejune, pursuen, subduen, triune; importune, opportune; inopportune. (Compare -ōōn, and, under same heading, -ūne.)

-ung: bung, clung, dung, flung, hung, lung, rung, slung, sprung, strung, stung, sung, swung, tongue, wrung, young; among, highstrung, Shantung, unhung, unstrung, unsung; overhung, underslung.

-unge(j): lunge, plunge, sponge; expunge.

-unk: bunk, chunk, drunk, dunk, flunk, funk, hunk, junk, monk, plunk, punk, shrunk, skunk, slunk, spunk, stunk, sunk, trunk; kerplunk, quidnunc.

-unt: blunt, brunt, bunt, front, grunt, hunt, lunt, punt, runt, shunt, stunt; affront, confront, forefront.

-up: crup, cup, pup, sup, tup, up; hiccup, makeup, setup, teacup, tossup; buttercup, develop, lovingcup.

-ūpe: drupe, dupe. (See -ōōp.)

-upt: abrupt, corrupt, disrupt, erupt; incorrupt, interrupt. (And preterites of words in -up, as in "cupped".)

-ûr: See êr.

-ûrb: See -êrb.

-ûrd: See -êard.

-ure: cure, dure, lure, Muir, pure, sure, your,
you're; abjure, adjure, allure, brochure,
cocksure, coiffure, demure, endure, ensure,
impure, inure, manure, mature, obscure,
perdure, procure, secure, unmoor, unsure;
amateur, aperture, armature, calenture,
comfiture, conoisseur, coverture, curvature,
cynosure, forfeiture, furniture, immature,
insecure, manicure, overture, paramour,
pedicure, premature, quadrature, reassure,
reinsure, signature, sinecure, tablature,
troubador, vestiture; caricature, discomfi-
ture, divestiture, entablature, expenditure,
investiture, literature, miniature, tempera-
ture; primogeniture. (See -ôor, also -ewêr
in two-syllable rhymes.)

-ûrf: See êrf.

-ûrge: See -êrge.

-ûrk: See -êrk.

-ûrl: See -êarl.

-ûrn: See -êarn.

-ûrp: See îrp.

-ûrse: See -êrce.

-ûrst: See -îrst.

-urt: See -êrt.

-ûrve: See -êrve.

-ûrze: furze, thyrse. (And add "s" to words in -êr, -îr and -ûr.)

-us, -uss: bus, buss, cuss, fuss, Gus, Hus, muss, plus, pus, Russ, thus, truss, us; cirrus, discuss, nimbus, nonplus, percus, Remus, stratus, abacus, Angelum, animus, blunderbuss, emulus. (And nearly 300 false, rhymes in words of two syllables and over, which end in -us and -ous. Thus "sarcopgagus", "bulbous", and "impetuous".)

-ūse: See -ûce.

-ūse (ūze): blues, fuse, fuze, mews, muse, news, use (verb); abuse, accuse, amuse, bemuse, confuse, contuse, diffuse, disuse, enthuse, excuse, infuse, misuse, peruse, refuse, suffuse, transfuse; disabuse, Syracuse. (See -ew, -ieu, -ūe and -ōō for plurals of nouns and third person singulars of verbs as in "pews", "adieus", and "blues".)

-ush: bush, "cush" (billiards), push, shush, swoosh; ambush; bramblebush, Hindu Kush.

-ush (as in "blush"): blush, brush, crush, flush, frush, gush, hush, lush, mush, plush, rush, slush, thrush, tush; outblush, outrush, uprush.

-usk: brusque, busk, dusk, fusc, husk, lusk,

93

musk, rusk, tusk, Usk; adusk, dehusk, sub-fusk.

-ust: bust, crust, dost, dust, gust, just, lust, must, rust, thrust, trust; adjust, adust, august, August, combust, disgust, distrust, encrust, entrust, incrust, mistrust, piecrust, robust, stardust, unjust, untrussed. (And preterites in -uss, as in "fussed".)

-ut, -utt: but, butt, crut, cut, glut, gut, hut, jut, Kut, mutt, nut, phut, putt, rut, scut, shut, slut, smut, strut, tut; abut, astrut, besmut, catgut, clear-cut, englut, gamut, outshut, peanut, rebut, woodcut; betel-nut, cocoanut, halibut, Lilliput, occiput, surre-but, waterbutt. (For rhymes to "put", see -oot.)

-ūte: beaut, boot, brute, Butte, chute, coot, cute, flute, fruit, hoot, jute, loot, lute, moot, mute, newt, root, route, scoot, scute, shoot, snoot, soot, suit, toot. Ute; acute, argute, astute, cahoot, cheroot, commute, compute, confute, depute, dilute, dispute, emeute, en-root, en route, galoot, hirsute, imbrute, im-pute, minute, outshoot, permute, pollute, pursuit, recruit, refute, repute, salute, sol-ute, unboot, unroot, uproot, volute; absolute, arrowroot, attribute, baldicoot, constitute, destitute, disrepute, dissolute, institute, involute, overshoot, prosecute, prostitute, resolute, substitute. (See -ōōt and, under

94

same heading, -ūte.)

-ūth: See -ōōth.

-ux, -ucks: Bucks, crux, dux, flux, lux, shucks, tux; conflux, efflux, influx, reflux. (And plurals of nouns and third person singulars of verbs in -uck, as in "ducks", "mucks".)

-uz: buzz, coz, does, doz., fuzz, Luz, muzz, Uz; abuzz.

-y(ī): ay, aye, buy, by, bye, cry, die, dry, eye, fie, fly, fry, guy, Guy, hi!, hie, high, I, lie, lye, my, nigh, phi, pi, pie, ply, pry, psi, rye, Rye, shy, sigh, sky, Skye, sly, spry, spy, sty, Thai, thigh, thy, tie, try, vie, why, wry, Wye; ally, apply, awry, belie, comply, decry, defy, descry, espy, go-by, good-bye, hereby, imply, July, magpie, mudpie, outcry, outvie, popeye, rely, reply, Shanghai, shoofly, standby, supply, thereby, untie, whereby; alibi, alkali, amplify, beatify, beautify, brutify, butterfly, candify, certify, clarify, classify, codify, crucify, damnify, dandify, dignify, edify, falsify, firefly, fortify, fructify, gasify, genii, glorify, gratify, horrify, hushaby, justify, lignify, liquefy, lullaby, magnify, modify, mollify, mortify, multiply, mystify, notify, nullify, occupy, ossify, petrify, purify, qualify, ramify, rarefy, ratify, rectify, sanctify, satisfy, scarify, signify, simplify, specify, stupefy, terrify, testify, torpify, typify, underlie, unify,

verbify, verify, versify, vilify, vivify; an-
gelify, disqualify, dissatisfy, exemplify, fos-
silify, identify, indemnify, intensify, per-
sonify, preoccupy, revivify, solidify.

-yle: See -īle.

-yme: See -īme.

-ÿmph: lymph, nymph.

-yne: See -īne.

-ÿnx: See -inx.

-ÿp: See -ip.

-yre: See -ire.

-ÿst: See -ist.

-ÿpse: See -ipse.

-yre: See -īre.

-yrrh: See -êr.

-ÿsm: See -ism.

-ÿst: See -ist.

-ÿth: See -ith.

-ythe: See -īthe.

-yve: See -īve.

-ÿx: See -ix.

TWO OR MORE SYLLABLE RHYMES

-abàrd: jabbered, scabbard, slabbered, tabard.

-abble: babble, cabble, dabble, drabble, gabble, rabble, scrabble; bedabble, bedrabble. (For rhymes to "squabble", see -obble.)

-abböt: abbot, Cabot, jabot, sabot.

-abbey, -abby: abbey, cabby, crabby, flabby, scabby, shabby, tabby. (And extend -ab for such rhymes as "cabby".)

-ābèl: See -āble.

-abid: rabid, tabid.

-ābiàn, -ābiön: fabian, gabion, Sabian, Arabian.

-ābiēs: babies, gabies, Jabez, rabies, scabies.

-abit: habit, rabbet, rabbit; cohabit, inhabit.

-āble, -ābèl: Abel, able, Babel, babel, cable, fable, gable, label, Mabel, sable, stable, table; disable, enable, unable, unstable.

-ābör, -ābêr: caber (Scotch), labor, neighbor, saber, tabor; belabor.

-äbrà: candelabra.

-āby: baby, gaby, maybe.

-acà: "bacca", dacca, paca, alpaca, malacca, polacca. (Compare -ackêr.)

-ācènt, -āscént: jacent, naissant, nascent; adjacent, complacent, complaisant, renais-

97

sant, renascent, subjacent; interjacent, superjacent.

-acét: See -assét.

-ācial: facial, glacial, racial, spatial; abbatial, palatial.

-ācious, -ātious: gracious, spacious; audacious, bibacious, bulbaceous, capacious, cetaceous, cretaceous, disgracious, edacious, fallacious, feracious, flirtatious, fugacious, herbaceous, Horatius, Ignatius, linguacious, loquacious, mendacious, minacious, misgracious, mordacious, predaceous, procacious, pugnacious, rampacious, rapacious, sagacious, salacious, sebaceous, sequacious, setaceous, tenacious, ungracious, veracious, vexatious, vivacious, voracious; carbonaceous, contumacious, disputatious, efficacious, execratious, farinaceous, incapacious, ostentatious, perspicacious, pertinacious, resinaceous, violaceous.

-ācis, -āsis: basis, crasis, glacis, phasis; oasis. (Compare plurals in -ēce.)

-ackáge: package, stackage, trackage.

-ackén: blacken, bracken, slacken.

-ackêr, -acquêr: backer, blacker, cracker, hacker, lacquer, packer, hijacker, quacker, slacker, stacker.

-ackét: bracket, jacket, packet, placket, racket, tacket.

-ackey, -acky: baccy, blackie, Jacky, knacky,

Lackey, quacky, tacky, wacky.

-ackle: cackle, crackle, grackle, hackle, macle, quackle, shackle, tackle; ramshackle.

-actêr, -actör: actor, factor, tractor; abstractor, attracter, character, compacter, contractor, detractor, distracter, enacter, exacter, extracter, infractor, olfactor, protractor, refractor, retractor, subtracter, transactor; benefactor.

-actic: lactic, tactic; didactic, emphractic, galactic, syntactic; prophylactic.

-actice: cactus, practice.

-actile: dactyle (or dactyl), tactile, tractile; contractile, protractile, retractile.

-action: action, faction, fraction, paction, taction, traction; abstraction, attraction, coaction, compaction, contaction, contraction, detraction, distraction, exaction, extraction, impaction, inaction, infraction, protraction, reaction, refraction, retraction, stupefaction, subaction, subtraction, transaction; arefaction, benefaction, calefaction, counteraction, interaction, labefaction, liquefaction, malefaction, petrifaction, putrefaction, rarefaction, retroaction, satisfaction; dissatisfaction.

-active: active, tractive; abstractive, attractive, coactive, distractive, enactive, inactive,

protractive, reactive, refractive, retractive;
calefactive, counteractive, purifactive, pu-
trefactive, retroactive, stupefactive.

-actly: compactly, exactly; matter-of-factly.

-actrèss: actress, factress; benefactress, de-
tractress, malefactress.

-acture: facture, fracture; compacture, manu-
facture.

-ācy: Casey, Gracie, lacy, Macy, racy, Tracy.

-ädà: Dada; armada, haggada, Nevada.

-adàm: Adam, madam; macadam.

-addèn: bad'un, gladden, madden, sadden;
engladden.

-addêr: adder, bladder, gadder, gladder, lad-
der, madder, padder, sadder; stepladder.
(See -attêr.)

-addèst, -addist: fadist, gladdest, maddest,
saddest; invadest. (See -attèst.)

-addle: addle, faddle, paddle, raddle, saddle,
spraddle, straddle; skedaddle, unsaddle.
(See -attle.)

-addöck: Braddock, haddock, Maddock, pad-
dock, shaddock.

-addy: caddy, daddy, faddy, laddie, paddy;
sugar daddy.

-ādèn, -āidèn: Aden, Haydn, laden, maiden;
mermaiden, overladen, unladen.

-ādêr: aider, trader; crusader, evader. (See -āter.)

-adgêr: badger, cadger.

-ādiênt: gradient, radiant.

-adish, -addish: baddish, caddish, faddish, gaddish, maddish, radish, saddish.

-ādium: radium, stadium, palladium.

-ādle: cradle, ladle; encradle.

-ädō: bravado, Mikado, passado; avocado, desperado, Colorado.

-ädō: dado; crusado, grenado, stoccado, tornado; bastinado, renegado.

-ädre: cadre, padre.

-ādy, ādi: Brady, braidy, cadi, glady, lady, maidie, O'Brady, Sadie, shady; landlady.

-āfêr: safer, wafer.

-àffêr, -àffīr, -aughêr: chaffer, gaffer, Kaffir, laugher, quaffer; cinematographer, photographer.

-affic: graphic, "maffick", traffic; autographic, lithographic, paragraphic, phonographic, photographic, pornographic, seismographic, telegraphic; autobiographic, cinematographic.

-affle: baffle, gaffle, raffle, snaffle.

-affled, -afföld: baffled, raffled, scaffold, snaffled.

-affy: baffy, chaffy, daffy, draffy, taffy.

-aftêr: after, dafter, grafter, laughter, rafter, shafter, wafter; hereafter, thereafter; thereinafter.

-ägá, -ägêr (hard): lager, saga.

-āgêr, -ājôr: cager, gauger, major, pager, sager, stager; assuager, presager, wager.

-aggárd: blackguard, baggard, haggard, laggard, staggered, swaggered.

-aggêr: bagger, bragger, dagger, flagger, gagger, jagger, nagger, ragger, tagger, wagger; carpet-bagger.

-aggish: haggish, naggish, waggish.

-aggle: draggle, gaggle, haggle, raggle, straggle, waggle; bedraggle.

-aggöt, -agáte: agate, Baggot, faggot, maggot.

-aggy, -aggie: Aggie, baggy, craggy, jaggy, knaggy, laggy, Maggie, quaggy, raggy, scraggy, shaggy, snaggy, swaggy, waggy.

-agic: magic, tragic; ellagic, pelagic.

-agile: agile, fragile.

-āgō: dago, sago; farrago, lumbago, Tobago, virago.

-ägō: farrago, Chicago.

-agön: dragon, flagon, wagon; snap-dragon.

102

-āgrànt: flagrant, fragrant, vagrant; infragrant.

-agship: flagship, hagship.

-āic: algebraic, archaic, Hebraic, Judaic, mosaic, prosaic, sodaic, trochaic; paradisaic.

-āidén: See -ādén:

-āiety, āity: gaiety, laity.

-āiler: gaoler. (And extend -ail for "jailer", "sailor", etc.)

-āiliff: bailiff, Caliph.

-āiling: ailing, grayling, paling. (And extend -āil for "prevailing", etc.)

-āilmént, -álemént: (Extend -āil, -āle for "ailment", "regalement", etc.)

-āily, -āly: bailey, bailie, daily, Daly, gaily, mailly, palely, scaly, shaly, snaily, stalely, vale; shillelagh, ukelele.

-āimént, -āymént: claimant, clamant, payment, raiment; defrayment, displayment, repayment.

-āindêr: attainder, remainder.

-āinful, -āneful: baneful, gainful, painful; disdainful.

-āinly: gainly, mainly, plainly, sanely, vainly; humanely, inanely, insanely, mundanely, profanely, ungainly, urbanely.

-āintêr: fainter, painter, tainter.

-āintly: faintly, quaintly, saintly.

-āinty: dainty, fainty,

-āiny: brainy, drainy, grainy, rainy, veiny,
zany; "champagney", Delaney.

-āiry, -āry: airy, chary, dairy, eyrie, fairy,
Gary, hairy, Mary, merry, nary, prairie,
scary, snary, vary, wary; canary, contrary,
vagary; Tipperary, voluntary; confection-
ary. (False rhymes, such as "bury", etc.)

-āisêr: See -azör.

-āisin: See -āzèn.

-āisy: See -āzy.

-āitèn, -ātàn: Dayton, Leyton, Satan,
straighten, straiten.

-āitêr: See -ātêr.

-āithful: faithful, scatheful.

-āitrèss: creatress, traitress, waitress.

-ājör: See -āgèr.

-ākèn, -ācön: bacon, shaken, waken; mis-
taken; undertaken.

-ākèr, -ācre: acher, acre, baker, breaker,
faker, fakir, maker, Quaker, raker, shaker,
taker, waker; bookmaker, peacemaker,
wiseacre.

-akō, -accō: Jacko, shako; tobacco.

104

-āky: achey, Blaikie, braky, flaky, quaky, shaky, snaky.

-alá: Bala, gala, Scala, cicala. (See **-arlêr.**)

-aláce, -allous: callous, chalice, Dallas, palace, Pallas, phallus. (Compare **-alice.**)

-alád, -allád: ballad, salad.

-alánce: balance, valance.

-ălder: alder, balder, Calder, scalder.

-ălding: balding, scalding, Spalding.

-aláte, -allét, -allöt: ballot, mallet, palate, pallet, shallot, valet.

-āliá: dahlia, Thalia; Australia, interalia, regalia, Westphalia.

-alice: Alice, chalice, malice. (See **-aláce.**)

-alid, -allied: calid, dallied, pallid, rallied, sallied, tallied, valid; invalid (adj.).

-āliph: See **-ailiff.**

-ălker, -ăwker, -ôrker: (Extend **-ălk, -ăwk, -ôrk.**)

-allánt: gallant, talent.

-ăller, -ăwler: (Extend **-ăll, -ăwl.**)

-allét: See **-aláte.**

-allic: Alec, Gallic, phallic; medallic, metallic, vandallic.

-ăllmént: appallment, installment.

-alliön: galleon, scallion, stallion; battalion, medallion, rapscallion.

-ällish: Dawlish, Gaulish, smallish, tallish.

-allön: Alan, Allen, gallon, Stalin, talon.

-allöp: gallop, jalap, scallop, shallop.

-ällöp, -ollöp: dollop, gollop, scallop, trollop, wallop.

-al'ör: pallor, valor.

-allow: aloe, callow, fallow, hallow, mallow, Mallow, sallow, shallow, tallow; marshmallow. (Add "s" to the above for "gallows".)

-ally: alley, bally, challis, dally, galley, pally, rally, sally, Sally, tally, valley; O'Malley, reveille, shilly-shally. (A number of false rhymes by wrongly accentuating last two syllables of certain adverbs, such as "principally".)

-ämá: Brahma, drama, lama, llama, mamma, pajama, Rama; Alabama, melodrama, panorama, Yokahama. (See -älmêr and -ärmêr.)

-älmêr: calmer, palmer; embalmer, salaamer. (See -ämá and -ärmêr.)

-älmêst, -älmist: calmest, palmist, psalmist; embalmist.

-almön: See -ammön.

-älmy: See -ärmy.

-ältár, -ältêr, -äultêr: altar, alter, falter,

106

halter, Malta, palter, psalter, salter, vaulter, Walter; assaulter, defaulter, drysalter, exalter, Gibraltar, unalter.

-ăltry: paltry, psaltery, drysaltery.

-ălty, -ăulty: faulty, malty, salty, vaulty, walty.

-ambeau, -ambō: ambo, crambo, flambeau, Sambo, zambo.

-ambêr: amber, camber, clamber, tambour, timbre. (See -ammêr.)

-ambit: ambit, gambit.

-amble: amble, bramble, Campbell, gamble, gambol, ramble, scamble, scramble, shamble, wamble; preamble.

-ambō: See -ambeau.

-āmeful: blameful, flameful, shameful.

-amél: camel, mammal, trammel; enamel.

-āmely: gamely, namely, lamely, tamely.

-amine: famine, gamin, stamin; examine, cross-examine.

-amlét: camlet, hamlet, Hamlet, samlet.

-ammăr, -ammêr, -amör: clamor, dammer, gammer, glamor, grammar, hammer, stammer, yammer; enamor, windjammer. (And extend -am for "crammer". See -ambêr.)

-ammön, -almön: gammon, mammon, salmon, backgammon.

-ammy: clammy, damme, drammie, gammy, hammy, jammy, mammy, Sammy, tammy, whammy.

-āmous, -āmus: famous, hamous, squamous; mandamus, ignoramus.

-ampèr: camper, champer, clamper, cramper, damper, hamper, pamper, ramper, scamper, stamper, tamper, tramper, vamper; decamper.

-ample: ample, sample, trample; example.

-ampus: campus, grampus, pampas, wampus.

-anä: Anna; banana, bandanna, Diana, Havana, iguana, Montana, Nirvana; Indiana, Juliana; Americana, Louisiana.

-anàte: See -anèt.

-ancèr, -answèr: answer, cancer, chancer, dancer, lancer, prancer; advancer, enhancer, romancer; geomancer, necromancer.

-ancét, -ansit: lancet, transit; Narragansett.

-anchor, -ancour: See -anker.

-ancid: fancied, rancid.

-ancy: chancy, fancy, Nancy; aeromancy, arithimancy, chiromancy, geomancy, hesitancy, lithomancy, mendicancy, necromancy, occupancy, onomancy, pyromancy, romancy, sycophancy, termagancy, vagrancy.

-anda: panda, propaganda, Uganda. (Compare **-andêr.**)

-andàl: See **-andle.**

-andàm, -andèm, -andöm: granddam, random, tandem; desperandum, memorandum.

-ander, -andor: blander, brander, candour, dander, gander, glander, grander, hander, pander, slander, stander ; Alexander, commander, coriander, demander, expander, gerrymander, Leander, Lysander, meander, oleander, philander, pomander, reprimander, salamander. (Compare **-antêr.**)

-andid, -anded: candid, uncandid. (Extend **-and.** Compare **-andied.**)

-andiēd: bandied, brandied, candied, dandied.

-andier, -andeur: bandier, candier, grandeur, handier, sandier. (Extend **-andy.**)

-andish: blandish, brandish, grandish, standish; outlandish.

-andit: bandit, pandit.

-andle, -andàl: candle, dandle, Handel, handle, Randall, sandal, scandal, vandal; mishandle.

-andlér: candler, chandler, dandler, handler ; tallow-chandler.

-andöm: See **-andàm.**

-andör: See **-andêr.**

-andrél, -andril: band-drill, hand-drill, mandrel, mandrill.

-andy: Andy, bandy, brandy, candy, dandy, Gandhi, handy, Kandy, Mandy, pandy, randy, sandy, Sandy, shandy, organdie, unhandy.

-anél, -anil, -annél: anil, cannel, channel, flannel, panel, scrannel; empanel.

-ānêr, āinêr: Extend -āne, -āin.

-āney, -āiney: Extend -āin, -āne.

-anét, -annét, -anite: gannet, granite, Janet, planet, Thanet: pomegranate.

-angêr (hard "g"): anger, angor, banger, Bangor, clangor, ganger, hangar, hanger, languor; haranguer.

-angêr (soft "g"): changer, danger, Grainger, granger, manger, ranger, stranger; arranger, endanger; disarranger, interchanger.

-angle: angle, bangle, dangle, jangle, mangle, rangle, spangle, strangle, tangle, twangle, wangle, wrangle; entangle, triangle, untangle; disentangle.

-angled, -anglêr, -angling. (Adapt above.)

-angō: mango, tango; contango, fandango; Pago Pago.

-anguish: anguish, languish.

-anic, -annic: Alnwick, panic, stannic, tannic; botanic, Britannic, galvanic, Germanic, mechanic, organic, Romanic, Satanic, titanic, tyrannic, volcanic, vulcanic; charlatanic, diaphanic, oceanic.

-anièl, -annuàl: annual, Daniel, granule, manual, spaniel; Emmanuel, Nathaniel.

-anish, -annish: banish, clannish, Danish, mannish, planish, Spanish, vanish; evanish.

-ankàrd, -ankered, -anchöred: anchored, bankered, cankered, hankered, tankard.

-ankêr, -anchör, -ancör: anchor, blanker, canker, hanker, rancor. (And extend -ank for "banker", etc.)

-ankle: ankle, rankle.

-ankly: Extend -ank.

-anky: Frankie, hanky, thankee, Yankee. (Extend -ank for "swanky", etc.)

-anly: Cranleigh, Hanley, manly, Stanley; unmanly.

-annà, -annàh:. anna, Anna, Hannah, manna; Havana, hosannah, Savannah, Susannah. (Compare -anà and -annêr.)

-annêr, -anör: banner, canner, manner, manor, spanner, tanner. (And extend -an for "fanner", etc.)

-annèx: annex, panics; galvanics, mechanics.

-anön: anon, canon, cannon, Shannon.

-anny: Annie, branny, canny, cranny, Fanny,

granny, mannie, nanny; uncanny.

-ansack: Anzac, ransack.

-ansion: mansion, panchion, scansion, stanchion; expansion.

-ansöm, -andsöme: handsome, hansom, ransom; transom; unhandsome.

-answêr: See **-ancêr.**

-antàm, -antöm: bantam, phantom.

-ante, -anti, -anty; ante, anti, auntie, chanty, Dante, pantie, scanty, shanty; Bacchante, Chianti; dilettante.

-antèl: See **-antle.**

-antêr: banter, canter, cantor, chanter, granter, grantor, panter, planter, ranter, scanter; decanter, displanter, enchanter, implanter, recanter, supplanter, transplanter.

-anthêr: anther, panther.

-antic: antic, frantic; Atlantic, corybantic, gigantic, pedantic, romantic; geomantic, sycophantic, transatlantic.

-antīle: infantile. (Compare **-ile.**)

-antle: cantle, mantel, mantle, scantle; dismantle.

-antlêr: antler, mantler, pantler; dismantler.

-antling: bantling, mantling, scantling; dismantling.

-antō, -anteau: canto, coranto, panto; Esperanto, Lepanto, portmanteau.

-antöm: See -antàm.

-anty: See -antė.

-antry: Bantry, chantry, gantry, pantry.

-annual: See -aniél.

-any: See -enny.

-āny: brainy, chaney, grainy, Janie, rainy, zany.

-anyàrd: lanyard, Spaniard, tan-yard.

-anzà: stanza; bonanza; Sancho Panza; extravaganza. ("Kansas" for plurals.)

-āpàl: See -āple.

-apél: See -apple.

-āpèn, -āpön: capon; misshapen, unshapen.

-āpêr, -āpîr, -āpör: caper, draper, paper, taper, tapir, vapor; newspaper, sandpaper. (Extend -ape.)

-aphic: See -affic.

-apid: rapid, sapid, vapid.

-āpist: papist, rapist; escapist, landscapist, redtapist.

-āple, -āpàl: capel, maple, papal, staple.

-aplèss: capless, chapless, hapless, napless,

113

sapless, strapless, tapless, **wrapless**.

-apling, -appling: dappling, grappling, knappling, sapling.

-apnèl: grapnel, shrapnel.

-äpör: See -äpêr.

-appèr: dapper. Extend **-ap**.

-appèt: lappet, tappet.

-apple, -apèl: apple, chapel, dapple, grapple, knapple, rappel, scapple, scrapple, **thrapple**; pineapple.

-appy: chappie, flappy, gappy, happy, knappy, nappy, sappy, scrappy, snappy; serape, slap-happy, unhappy.

-aptêr, -aptör: apter, captor, chapter; adapter, adoptor, recaptor.

-aption: caption; adaption, collapsion, contraption, recaption.

-aptist, aptèst: aptest, Baptist, raptest; adaptest, inaptest; anabaptist.

-apture: capture, rapture; enrapture, recapture.

-aràb: arab, Arab, scarab.

-aräge: barrage, garage.

-ärbêr, -ärbör: arbor, barber, harbor; unharbor.

-ärbêred, -ärböard: barbered, harbored, lar-

114

board, starboard.

-ärble, -ärbél: barbel, garble, marble, warble.

-ärcél: parcel, sarcel, tarsal, varsal; meta-
tarsal.

-ärchêr: archer, marcher, parcher, starcher;
departure.

-ärchy: See -arky.

-ärchy (soft "ch"): Archy, larchy, starchy,
Karachi.

-ärdén, -ärdön: Arden, garden, harden, par-
don; beergarden, bombardon, caseharden,
enharden, roularden.

-ärdêr: ardor, carder, harder, larder; bom-
barder, Cunarder.

-ärdy: hardy, lardy, mardy, tardy; foolhardy,
Lombardy, Picardy. (Compare -ärty.)

-âréä: area; Bavaria, Bulgaria, wistaria;
Berengaria.

-arél, -arrél, -aröl: barrel, carol, Carroll, Dar-
rell, apparel. ("Harold" for past tense.)

-ârely: barely, fairly, rarely, squarely, yarely;
unfairly; debonairly.

-ârêm, -ârum: Aram, harem, Sarum; harum-
scarum.

-arénce: Clarence, transparence. (Also -ant,
-ent + "s".)

115

-arét, -arát, -arrét -arröt: arret, Baratt, carat, caret, carrot, claret, garret, karat, parrot.

-ärgent: argent, sergeant.

-ärgêr: charger, larger; enlarger.

-ärging: barging, charging; discharging, enlarging; overcharging.

-ärgō, -ärgōt: Argo, argot, cargo, Dargo, largo, Margot; botargo, embargo, Wells Fargo; supercargo.

-âriês: charier, hairier, warier.

-âriàn, -âryàn: Arian, aryan; agrarian, Bavarian, barbarian, Bulgarian, caesarean, grammarian, librarian, Rotarian, vulgarian; centenarian, proletarian; abecedarian, disciplinarian, predestinarian; valetudianarian. (Compare -ariön.)

-ariàt, -ariöt: chariot, Harriet, lariat, Marriott, Marryatt; Iscariot.

-âric: baric, carrick, Garrick; Amharic, barbaric, Bulgaric, Megaric, pimaric, Pindaric, polaric, saccharic, stearic, tartaric; Balearic, cinnabaric.

-arice, -arris: Clarice, Farris, Harris, Paris; phalaris, polaris.

-arid, -arried: arid, carried, harried, married, parried, tarried, varied; miscarried, remarried, unmarried, unvaried; intermarried.

-âring, -âiring, -eāring: bearing, glaring.
(Extend -âre, -âir, -eār.)

-ariön, -arriön: carrion, clarion, Marion; Hilarion. (Compare -ariàn.)

-arious: Darius, Marius, various; Aquarius, bifarious, contrarious, gregarious, hilarious, nefarious, ovarious, precarious, vicarious; multifarious, Sagittarius, temerarious.

-ârish, -eārish: barish, bearish, fairish, garish, perish, rarish, sparish, squarish; debonarish.

-arity: charity, clarity, parity, rarity; vulgarity; angularity, jocularity, popularity, regularity, secularity, similarity, singularity; dissimilarity, irregularity, particularity; perpendicularity.

-ärkén: darken hearken.

-ärkêr: (Extend -ärk. Compare "parka".)

-ärkét: market; Newmarket.

-ärkish: darkish, larkish, sparkish.

-ärkle: darkle, sparkle; monarchal; matriarchal, patriarchal.

-ärkling: darkling, sparkling.

-ärkly: darkly, sparkly, starkly.

-ärky: barky, darkie, heark'ee, larky, marquee, parky, sparky, Starkey; malarkey; heterarchy, hierarchy, matriarchy, oligar-

117

chy, patriarchy.

-ärlêr, -ärlör: gnarler, marler, parlor, snarler; Transvaaler.

-ärlét: carlet, harlot, scarlet, starlit, varlet.

-ärley, -ärly: barley, Charlie, gnarly, Marley, parley, snarly. (Extend -är for "particularly", etc.)

-ärlic: garlic, Harlech, sarlyk; pilgarlick.

-ärling: darling, marling, snarling, sparling, starling. (Extend -ärl.)

-ärlōw: Barlow, Carlow, Harlow, Marlow.

-ärly: See -ärley.

-ärmêr, -ärmör: armor, charmer, farmer, harmer; alarmer, disarmer, plate-armor.

-ärmèst, -ärmist: alarmist. (Extend -ärm. Compare -älmist.)

-ärmy, -älmy: army, balmy, barmy, psalmy, smarmy.

-ärnâl, -arnèl: carnal, charnel, darnel, Farnol.

-ärnêr: darner, garner, yarner.

-ärnéss: farness, harness.

-ärnét: Barnet, garnet; incarnate.

-ärnëy: barney, blarney, Carney; Killarney.

-ärnish: barnish, garnish, tarnish, varnish.

118

-arön: Arran, baron, barren, Charon, marron, Sharon; fanfaron, McLaren.

-ärpêr: carper, harper, scarper, sharper.

-arräck: arrack, barrack, carrack. (See **-aric.**)

-arränt: arrant, parent; apparent, transparent.

-ärrànt, -orrènt: torrent, warrant; abhorrent.

-arràs: arras, Arras, harass; embarrass. (See **-aris.**)

-arrêl: See **-arêl.**

-ärrêl: See **-oràl.**

-arrèn: See **-arön.**

-ärrén: florin, foreign, sporran; warren.

-arriáge, -aráge: carriage, marriage; disparage, miscarriage, mismarriage; intermarriage.

-arriêr: barrier, carrier, charier, farrier, harrier, marrier, parrier, tarrier.

-arried: See **-arid.** (Extend **-arry.**)

-ärriêr, -örriör: quarrier, sorrier, warrior.

-arriön: See **-ariön.**

-arrōw: arrow, barrow, Barrow, faro, farrow, harrow, Harrow, Jarrow, marrow, narrow, Pharoah, sparrow, taro, yarrow, Yarrow; bolero, dinero, pierrot, primero, sombrero, torero, vaquero; caballero, banderillero,

Embarcadero.

-arry: Barry, Carrie, carry, charry, harry, Harry, Larry, marry, parry, sari, scarry, sparry, starry, tarry; miscarry; hari-kari, intermarry.

-ärry: barry, charry, scarry, sparry, starry, tarry (from "tar"); Araçari, Carbonari.

-ärshàl, -ärtial: marshal, Marshall, martial, partial; immartial, impartial.

-ärsley: parsley, sparsely.

-ärsön: arson, Carson, parson, squarson.

-ärtàn, -ärtèn: barton, Barton, carton, hearten, marten, martin, Martin, smarten, Spartan, tartan; dishearten, enhearten; kindergarten.

-ärtàr, -ärtêr: barter, carter, charter, darter, garter, martyr, parter, smarter, starter, tartar, tarter; bemartyr, imparter, selfstarter, upstarter.

-ärtel: cartel.

-ärtful: artful, cartful, heartful.

-ärtial: See -ärchàl.

-ärtist, -ärtèst: artist, chartist, smartest. (Extend -ärt.)

-ärtle: dartle, startle.

-ärtlèt: Bartlett, chartlet, heartlet, martlet, partlet, tartlet.

120

-ärtly: partly, smartly, tartly.

-ärtnêr: heartener, partner, smartener; disheartener.

-ärtridge: cartridge, cart-ridge, partridge.

-ärty: arty, hearty, party, smarty; Astarte, ecarte, ex parte; Cancarty.

-ärture: See **-ärchêr.**

-ärvêl: carvel, Darvel, larvel, marvel.

-ärvêst: carvest, harvest, starvest.

-âry: See **-âiry.**

-äsàl, -äzél: basal, basil, hazel, nasal, phrasal; appraisal, witch hazel.

-ascàl, -aschàl: paschal, rascal.

-ascâr: See **-askêr.**

-äscênce: nascence; complacence, obeisance, renascence.

-äscênt: nascent, renascent. (See **-âcent.**)

-ascot: Ascot, mascot.

-äsemênt: basement, casement, placement; abasement, begracement, belacement, debasement, defacement, displacement, effacement, embracement, emplacement, enlacement, erasement; misplacement, replacement; interlacement.

-ashên, -ashion, -assion, -ation: ashen, fashion, passion, ration; compassion, dispassion.

-ashêr: Dasher, rasher; haberdasher. (And extend **-ash** for "masher", etc.)

-ashy: ashy, flashy, mashy, plashy, slashy, splashy, trashy.

-āsià: Asia, Dacia, fascia; acacia, Alsatia, Dalmatia, fantasia.

-āsian: Asian, abrasion, Caucasian, Eurasian, occasion, persuasion. (Compare **-ātion.**)

-āsin, -āsön, -āstèn: basin, caisson, chasten, hasten, Jason, mason.

-āsis: See **-ācis.**

-askêr, -ascà, -ascär: asker, basker, lascar, masker, tasker; Alaska, Nebraska, Madagascar.

-askét: basket, casket, flasket, gasket.

-aspêr: aspen, Caspar, clasper, gasper, grasper, jasper, Jasper, rasper. (Extend **-asp.**)

-assèl: castle, hassle, passel, tassel, vassal, wassail; entassel, envassal.

-asses: molasses. (Extend **-ass.**)

-assét, -acèt, -acit: asset, basset, facet, fascet, placet, tacit. (Compare **-acid.**)

-assic: classic, boracic, Jurassic, potassic, sebacic, thoracic, Triassic.

-assion: See **-ashèn.**

-assive: massive, passive; impassive.

-assle: See **-assèl**.

-assock: bassock, cassock, hassock.

-assy: brassie, brassy, chassis, classy, gassy, glace, glassy, grassy, Jassy, lassie, massy, passe, sassy; Coomassie, Malagasy, morassy, Tallahassee; Haile Selassie.

-astà: pasta. (Compare **-astêr**.)

-astàrd, -astêred: bastard, castored, dastard, mastered, plastered.

-āstén: See **-āsin**.

-astèn: fasten.

-astêr: aster, Astor, blaster, caster, castor, faster, master, pastor, plaster, vaster; bandmaster, beplaster, cadaster, disaster, schoolmaster, taskmaster; alabaster, burgomaster, criticaster, medicaster, oleaster, quartermaster.

-āstêr: baster, chaster, haster, paster, taster, waster; poetaster.

-astic: clastic, drastic, mastic, plastic, spastic; bombastic, dichastic, dynastic, elastic, emplastic, fantastic, gymnastic, monastic, proplastic, sarcastic, scholastic; amphiblastic, anaclastic, antiphrastic, bioplastic, ceroplastic, deutoplastic, docimastic, Hudibrastic, metaphrastic, neoplastic, onomastic, paraphrastic, periphrastic, phelloplastic, pleonastic, protoplastic, scholiastic; antono-

123

mastic, ecclesiastic, encomiastic, enthusiastic, iconoclastic, paronomastic.

-astle: See **-assèl.**

-astlý: ghastly, lastly, vastly; steadfastly.

-ãsty: hasty, pasty, tasty.

-asty: blasty, nasty, vasty.

-ãtà: beta, data, eta, strata, theta, zeta; albata, dentata, errata, pro rata, postulata, ultimata, vertebrata; invertebrata.

-atà: data, strata; pro rata; matamata, serenata.

-ätà: cantata, errata, regatta, sonata.

-ãtàl: datal, fatal, natal, Statal; prenatal, postnatal, antenatal.

-ãtàn: See **-ãitén**

-ãtànt, -ãtènt: blatant, latent, natant.

-atchèt: Datchet, hatchet, latchet, ratchet.

-ãtchmàn: Scotchman, watchman.

-atchy: batchy, patchy, scratchy; Apache.

-atènt: patent. (Compare **-atin.**)

-ãter, -ãtör: cater, crater, freighter, gaiter, greater, Hayter, later, mater, pater, straighter, traitor, waiter; creator, cunctator, curator, dictator, equator, scrutator, spectator, testator; alligator, carburetor, commentator, cónservator, valuator. (Extend **-ate** for about 200 other good rhymes.

124

Thus "bater", "navigator", etc.)

-athêr: blather, gather, lather, rather; fore-gather.

-äther: farther, father.

-āthing: See -āything.

-āthos: Athos, bathos, pathos.

-ātial: See -ācial.

-aki: khaki, saki.

-attic: attic, static; agnatic, aquatic, astatic, asthmatic, chromatic, climatic, commatic, dalmatic, dogmatic, dramatic, ecstatic, emphatic, erratic, fanatic, hepatic, hieratic, lavatic, mathematic, phlegmatic, piratic, pragmatic, prismatic, prostatic, quadratic, rheumatic, sabbatic, schematic, schismatic, sciatic, spermatic, stigmatic, thematic, traumatic; acrobatic, Adriatic, aerostatic, aromatic, Asiatic, autocratic, automatic, bureaucratic, diplomatic, emblematic, Hanseatic, hydrostatic, kinematic, operatic, pancreatic, plutocratic, problematic, symptomatic, thermostatic; anagrammatic, aristocratic, axiomatic, epigrammatic, idiocratic, idiomatic, melodramatic; idiosyncratic. (Compare -adic.)

-atin, -attèn: Latin, matin, patin, platen, satin; batten, fatten, flatten; Prestatyn.

-ation, ātian: nation, ration, station; ablation, aëration, agnation, aration, Asian, carnation, cassation, castration, causation, cessation, citation, collation, creation, cremation, crustacean, crustation, curvation, Dalmatian, delation, dentation, dictation, dilation, donation, duration, efflation, elation, equation, filtration, fixation, flirtation, flotation, formation, frustration, furcation, gestation, gradation, gunation, gustation, gyration, hortation, hydration, illation, inflation, lactation, laudation, laxation, legation, libation, location, lunation, migration, mutation, narration, negation, nervation, notation, novation, oblation, oration, ovation, palpation, pausation, phonation, placation, plantation, predation, privation, probation, prostration, pulsation, purgation, quotation, relation, rogation, rotation, saltation, salvation, sensation, serration, signation, stagnation, stellation, striation, sublation, tarnation, taxation, temptation, testacean, testation, titration, translation, vacation, venation, vexation, vibration, vocation; abdication, aberration, abjuration, abnegation, abrogation, acclamation, acclimation, accubation, accusation, activation, actuation, adaptation, adjudication, adjuration, admiration, adoration, adornation, adulation, advocation, affectation, affirma-

tion, aggeration, aggravation, aggregation,
agitation, allegation, alligation, allocation,
alteration, altercation, alternation, ambu-
lation, ampliation, amputation, angulation,
animation, annexation, annotation, annula-
tion, appellation, application, approbation,
arbitration, argentation, arrogation, aspi-
ration, assentation, assignation, attestation,
auguration, aviation, avocation, bifurcation,
blusteration, calcination, calculation, cam-
eration, cancellation, capitation, captiva-
tion, castellation, castigation, celebration,
cementation, cerebration, circulation, cogi-
tation, coloration, combination, commenda-
tion, compensation, compilation, complica-
tion, compurgation, computation, concen-
tration, condemnation, condensation, con-
donation, confirmation, confiscation, con-
flagration, conformation, confrontation,
confutation, congelation, congregation, con-
jugation, conjuration, connotation, conse-
cration, conservation, consolation, constella-
tion, consternation, consultation, conversa-
tion, convocation, copulation, coronation,
corporation, correlation, corrugation, crepi-
tation, crimination, culmination, cultivation,
cumulation, decimation, declamation, dec-
laration, declination, decoration, decrus-
tation, decussation, dedication, defalca-
tion, defamation, defecation, defloration,

degradation, degustation, delectation, delegation, demarcation, dementation, demonstration, denudation, deportation, depredation, deprivation, deputation, derivation, derogation, desecration, dessication, designation, desolation, destination, detestation, detonation, detruncation, devastation, deviation, digitation, disclamation, dislocation, dispensation, disputation, dissertation, dissipation, distillation, divagation, divination, domination, edentation, education, elevation, elongation, emanation, embarkation, embrocation, emendation, emulation, enervation, epuration, equitation, estimation, estivation, evagation, evocation, exaltation, exclamation, exculpation, execration, exhalation, exhortation, exhumation, expectation, expiation, expiration, expiscation, explanation, explication, exploitation, exploration, exportation, expugnation, expurgation, extirpation, extrication, exudation, exultation, exundation, fabrication, falcation, fascination, fecundation, federation, fenestration, fermentation, festimation, figuration, flagellation, flagitation, fluctuation, foliation, fomentation, forcipation, formication, fornication, fraternation, frumentation, fulmination, fumigation, furfuration, generation, germination, glaciation, glomeration, graduation, granulation, gratulation, gravitation, gubernation, habitation, hesitation, hibernation, humectation, ideation, illustration, imitation, immanation, immigration, immolation, impanation, implication, importation, imprecation, impregnation, imputation, incantation, incarnation, incertation, inchoation, incitation, inclination, incremation, incrustation, incubation, inculcation, inculpation, incurvation, indication, indignation, induration, inequation, infestation, infeudation, inflammation, information, inhalation, inhumation, innervation, innovation, insolation, intimation, intonation, inundation, incitation, inclination, incrassation, incremation, incrustation, incubation, inculcation, inculpation, incurvation, indentation, indication, indignation, induration, inequation, infestation, infeudation, infiltration, inflammation, information, inhalation, innervation, innovation, inspiration, installation, instigation, instillation, insufflation, insulation, integration, intensation, intonation, intrication, inundation, invitation, invocation, irrigation, irritation, isolation, jaculation, jubilation, laceration, lachrymation, lamentation, lamination, lapidation, laureation, legislation, levigation, levitation, liberation, limitation, lineation, liquidation, lubrication, lucubration, mac-

eration, machination, maculation, mallea-
tion, mediation, medication, meditation,
mensuration, ministration, moderation,
modulation, molestation, mutilation, nata-
tion, navigation, nictitation, nidulation,
nomination, numeration, obduration, obli-
gation, occulation, occupation, operation,
ordination, oscillation, oscitation, oscula-
tion, ostentation, oxidation, ozonation, pab-
ulation, pagination, palliation, palpitation,
peculation, penetration, percolation, per-
fectation, perforation, permeation, permu-
tation, pernoctation, peroration, perscruta-
tion, personation, perspiration, perturba-
tion, polliation, postillation, postulation,
predication, preparation, preservation,
proclamation, procreation, procuration, pro-
fanation, prolongation, promulgation, prop-
agation, propogation, provocation, publi-
cation, punctuation, racemation, radiation,
realization, recantation, recitation, recla-
mation, recreation, recubation, reformation,
refutation, regelation, registration, regula-
tion, relaxation, relocation, remonstration,
renovation, reparation, replication, repro-
bation, reservation, resignation, respiration,
restoration, retardation, revelation, revoca-
tion, reogation, rumination, rustication,
salication, salutation, satiation, saturation,
scintillation, separation, sequestration, sic-

cation, signation, simulation, situation, speculation, spoliation, sternutation, stimulation, stipulation, stridulation, stylobation, subjugation, sublevation, subligation, sublination, subluxation, subornation, subrogation, succusation, suffocation, sulphuration, suppuration, suspiration, sustenation, termination, titillation, titurbation, toleration, transformation, transmigration, transmutation, tribulation, trepidation, triplication, turbination, ulceration, ululation, undulation, usurpation, vacillation, validation, valuation, vegetation, veneration, ventilation, vesication, vindication, violation, visitation, vitiation, vulneration; abbreviation, abomination, accentuation, accumulation, administration, adulteration, agglomeration, alienation, alimentation, alleviation, alliteration, amalgamation, amplification, annihilation, annunciation, anticipation, appropriation, approximation, argumentation, articulation, asphyxiation, assassination, asseveration, assimilation, association, attenuation, authorization, brutalization, calumniation, canonization, capitulation, carbonization, carnifivation, civilization, clarification, classification, coagulation, codification, cognomination, cohabitation, colonization, columniation, commemoration, commensuration, commiseration, communication, concatenation, conciliation, confabulation, confederation, configuration, conglomeration, congratulation, consideration, consolidation, contamination, continuation, cooperation, co-ordination, corroboration, crystallization, debilitation, degeneration, delineation, denomination, denunciation, depopulation, depreciation, despoliation, determination, dignification, dilapidation, disapprobation, discoloration, disfiguration, disinclination, disintegration, disobligation, dissemination, dissimulation, dissociation, divarication, documentation, domestication, dulcification, ebonkfication, edification, edulcoration, effectuation, effemination, ejaculation, elaboration, elicitation, elimination, elucidation, elutriation, emaciation, emancipation, emasculation, enumeration, enunciation, equalization, equilibration, equivocation, eradication, etiolation, evacuation, evagination, evaporation, exacerbation, exaggeration, examination, exasperation, excoriation, excrusiation, exhilaration, exoneration, expatiation, expectoration, expostulation, expropriation, extenuation, extermination, facilitation, falsification, felicitation, ferrumination, fertilization, florification, fortification, fossilization, fructification, galvanization, gelatination, gesticulation, glorification, gratification, habilitation, habituation, hallucination, harmonization, Hellenization, horrification, humanization, humiliation, hypothecation, idealization, illiteration, illumination, imagination, immaculation, immoderation, impersonation, imperturbation, impropriation, improvisation, inaffectation, inanimation, inapplication, inauguration, incarceration, incineration, incorporation, incrimination, inebriation, infatuation, ingemination, initiation, inoculation, inosculation, insanitation, insemination, insinuation, interpolation, interpretation, interrogation, intoxication, investigation, irradiation, jollification, Judaization, justification, legalization, legitimation, licentiation, liquidation, manifestation, manipulation, masticulation, matriculation, melioration, mellification, misinformation, modernization, modification, mollification, moralization, mortification, multiplication, mystification, nasalization, negotiation, notification, nullification, obliteration, origination, organization, ossification, pacification, participation, perambulation, peregrination, perpetuation, petrification, polarization, precipitation, predestination, predomination, prefiguration, prejudication, premeditation, preoccupation, preponderation, prevarication, procrastination, prognostication, prolification, pronunciation, propitiation, protuberation, purification, qualification, ramification, ratification, recalcitration, reciprocation, reclimination, recommendation, recrimination, rectification, recuperation, refrigeration, regeneration, regurgitation, reiteration, reintegration, rejuvenation, remuneration, renunciation, representation, repudiation, resuscitation, retaliation, revivication, reverberation, sanctification, sanguification, scarification, signification, solemnization, solicitation, sophistication, specialization, specification, stabilization, stratification, stultification, sublineation, subordination, symbolization, tartarization, temporization, tergiversation, testamentation, thurification, tranquillization, triangulation, vaporization, variegation, vaticination, verbalization, vermiculation, versification, vigesimation, vilification, vitriolation, vituperation, vivification, vociferation; alcoholization, amelioration, beatification, circumnavigation, contra-indication, cross-examination, demonetization, deterioration, differentiation, discontinuation, disqualification, diversification, electrification, excommunication, exemplification, experimentation, extemporization, identification, inconsideration, indemnification, individuation, misrepresentation, naturalization, personification, predetermination, ratiocination, recapitulation, reconciliation, spiritualization, syllabification, tintinabulation, transubstantiation. (Also see -asion.)

-àtist: See -attèst.

-ātive: dative, native, sative, stative; collative, creative, dilative, translative; abrogative, aggregative, alterative, animative, approbative, cogitative, copulative, criminative, cumulative, decorative, deprecative, designative, dominative, duplicative, emanative, emulative, execrative, explicative, glutinative, gravitative, hesitative, imitative, implicative, incubative, innovative, irritative, iterative, lacerative, legislative, meditative, mitigative, operative, procreative, radiative, recreative, replicative, separative, stimulative, vegetative, violative; appreciative, associative, communicative, degenerative, deliberative, denunciative, discriminative, enumerative, enunciative, exonerative, imaginative, incogitative, incriminative, interpretative, manipulative, opinionative, participative, pronunciative, recuperative, retaliative, verificative, vituperative.

-atlèss: Atlas, fatless, hatless; cravatless.

-atling, -attling: battling, catling, fatling, gatling, ptattling, rattling, spratling, tattling; tittle-tattling.

-atly: fatly, flatly, patly, rattly.

-ātō: Cato, Plato ; potato, tomato.

-āto: chateau; legato, mulatto, tomato, staccato; obbligato, pizzicato; enamorato.

-ătŏr: See -ātêr.

-atrap: bat-trap, cat-trap, rat-trap, satrap.

-ātress: traitress, waitress; creatress, dictatress, spectatress, imitatress.

-ātrix: matrix; cicatrix, testatrix, spectatrix, testatrix; aviatrix, generatrix, imitatrix, mediatrix; administratrix, inpropriatrix.

-ātron: matron, natron, patron.

-atten: See -atin.

-attêr: attar, batter, blatter, chatter, clatter, fatter, flatter, hatter, latter, matter, patter, platter, ratter, satyr, scatter, shatter, smatter, spatter, splatter, tatter; bescatter, bespatter, Mad Hatter. (See -addêr, -atá.)

-attern, -aturn: pattern, Saturn, slattern.

-attêst, -atist, -atticed: bratticed, fattest, latticed, statist. (And extend -at for "flattest".)

-attle: battle, cattle, chattel, prattle, rattle, tattle; death-rattle, embattle, Seattle; tittle-tattle. (See -addle.)

-attlêr, -atlêr: battler, prattler, rattler, Statler, tattler. (Extend -attle, -addle.)

-attling: See -atling.

-attō, -atteau: chateau, gateau, plateau, mulatto.

-atty: batty, catty, chatty, fatty, gnatty, Hattie, matty, natty, Patti, patty, ratty, scatty; Cincinnati. (Compare **-addy**.)

-ātum: datum, stratum; eratum, pomatum, substratum; postulatum, ultimatum; desideratum, superstratum.

-āture: nature; good-nature, ill-nature, plicature, legislature, nomenclature.

-ature, -atchêr: stature. (There is no good rhyme to this but extensions of **-ach** and **-atch** may be permitted, as in "catcher".)

-ātus: status, stratus; afflatus,, hiatus, senatus; apparatus, literatus, saleratus.

-atus: gratis, lattice, status; apparatus.

-ātẏ, -eightẏ, -ateẏ: eighty, Haiti, Katie, matey, platy, praty, slaty, weighty.

-ăucêr: Chaucer, saucer. (Compare **-ôarsêr**.)

-ăucus: caucus, Dorcas, raucous.

-ăuction: auction; concoction, decoction.

-ăudàl: caudal, caudle, dawdle.

-ăudit: audit, plaudit.

-ăudẏ, -ăwdy: bawdy, dawdy, gaudy, Maudie. (See **-ăughty**.)

-auffêur: chauffeur, gopher, loafer, sofa.

-aughtêr (as in "laughter"): See **-aftêr**.

137

-ăughtêr: daughter, slaughter, tauter, man-
slaughter. (Compare -ôrtêr, -ôrdêr.)

-ăughty: haughty, naughty. (See -ăudy.)

-ăulic: aulic; hydraulic; interaulic. (Compare
-olic.)

-ăultêr: See -ăltàr.

-ăulty: faulty, malty, salty, vaulty, walty.

-ăundêr: launder, maunder.

-ăuntêr: chaunter, flaunter, gaunter, haunter,
jaunter, saunter, taunter, vaunter.

-auntie: See -antė.

-ăupêr: pauper. (Compare -ôrpör.)

-ăuseous, ăutious: cautious, nauseous; precau-
tious.

-ăusêr, -ăwsêr: causer, hawser, pauser, Mauser.

-ăustràl: austral, claustral.

-ăution: caution; precaution. (See -ōrtion.)

-ävà: Ava, guava, Java, lava, larva; cassava,
palaver. (Compare extensions of ärve.)

-avàge: lavage, ravage, savage, scavage.

-ävàl: naval, navel, cave-ale, Wavell.

-avėl: cavil, gavel, gravel, ravel, Savile,
travel; unravel.

-avėlin: javelin, ravelin.

-ävelÿ: bravely, gravely, knavely.

138

-āvemént: lavement, pavement; depravement, engravement, enslavement.

-āvén: craven, graven, haven, mavin, raven, shaven; engraven, New Haven.

-avêr: cadaver, palaver.

-āvêr: See -āvör.

-avêrn: cavern, tavern.

-āviour: clavier, pavior, saviour, Xavier; Batavia, behavior, Belgravia, Moravia.

-avid: avid, gravid, pavid; impavid.

-āvis: avis, Davis, mavis, Mavis; rara avis.

-avish: lavish, ravish; enravish, McTavish.

-āvish: bravish, knavish, slavish.

-āvör, -āvêr: favor, flavor, quaver, savor; disfavor; demiquaver, hemiquaver, semiquaver. (Extend **-āve** for "braver", etc.)

-āvy: cavy, Davy, gravy, navy, slavey, wavy.

-avvy: navvy, savvy.

-âwdry: Audrey, bawdry, tawdry.

-ăwdy: See -ăudy.

-ăwkêr: See -ălkêr.

-ăwful: awful, lawful; unlawful.

-ăwky, -ălky: gawky, pawky, "talkie"; Milwaukee. (Extend **-ălk** for "stalky".)

-ăwning: awning, dawning, fawning, spawn-

139

ing, yawning. (Extend -āwn. Compare -ôrning.)

-ăwny: brawny, fawny, lawny, Pawnee, sawney, scrawny, Shawnee, tawny, yawny; mulligatawny. (Compare -ôrny.)

-ăwyêr: foyer, lawyer, sawyer; topsawyer.

-axén, -axŏn: flaxen, Jackson, Saxon, waxen.

-axy: flaxy, Laxey, staxy, taxi, waxy; galaxy; ataraxy.

-āydāy, -eydāy: heyday, Mayday, payday, playday.

-āyêr, -eyôr: Mayor. (Extend -āy and -ey for "gayer", "surveyor". Compare -āre, -āir.)

-āymản: Bremen, cayman, Damon, drayman, flamen, Haman, layman, Lehman, Ramon, stamen; highwayman.

-āymềnt: claimant, payment, raiment; allayment, betrayment, defrayment, prepayment, repayment.

-āything: bathing, plaything, scathing, swathing.

-ăzả: Gaza, plaza, Zaza; piazza.

-azård: brassard, hazard, mazard; haphazard.

-āzél: See -āsản.

-āzén, -āzŏn, -āisin: blazon, brazen, glazen, raisin, scazon; emblazon; diapason.

-āzŏr, -āisêr: blazer, Fraser, gazer, lazar,

140

phraser, praiser, raiser, razer, razor; appraiser, dispraiser, self-praiser, star-gazer, upgazer, upraiser; paraphraser.

-āzier: brazier, crazier, glazier, hazier, lazier.

-āzön: See **-āsin.**

-āzy, āisy: crazy, daisy, Daisy, hazy, jasey, lazy, mazy, Maisie, quasi; lackadaisy.

-azzle: Basil, dazzle, drazil, frazzle, razzle; bedazzle, razzle-dazzle.

-ēá: Leah, Rhea, Zea; Althea, Crimea, Hygeia, idea, Korea, Judea, Maria, Medea, obeah, spirea; dahabeah, Dorothea, gonorrhea, Latakia, panacea, ratafia ; Cassiopea.

-ēachêr, -ēature, -ēechêr: creature, feature. (And extend ēach and -ēech.)

-ēabōard: keyboard, seaboard.

-ēachmênt: preachment; beseechment, impeachment.

-ēachy: beachy, beechy, bleachy, Nietzsche, peachy, preachy, reachy, queachy, reechy, screechy, speechy.

-ēacön: beacon, deacon, weaken; archdeacon.

-ēadêd: Extend -ēad, -ēat.

-eadên: deaden, Heddon, leaden, redden, Sedden, threaden; Armageddon.

-ēadêr, -ēdàr, -ēdêr, -ēedêr: cedar. (And extend -ēad, -ēde and -ēed.)

141

-ĕadle, -ēedle: beadle, Cheadle, daedal, needle, tweedle, wheedle; bipedal; centipedal, semipedal. (Compare -ēetle.)

-ĕadlock: deadlock, headlock, wedlock.

-ĕadwāy: dead-way, headway, Medway.

-ĕady: See -ĕddy.

-ēady: See -ēedy.

-ĕafêr: deafer, feoffor, heifer, zephyr; Strathpeffer, "whateffer".

-ĕafêst (ef): deafest, prefaced.

-ēafy, -ēefy: beefy, feoffee, Fifi, leafy, reefy, sheafy.

-ēagêr, -ēagre, -ēaguêr, -iguêr: eager, leaguer, meager, beleaguer, intriguer; overeager.

-ēagle, -ēgal: beagle, eagle, gragal, legal, regal, sea-gull; illegal, inveigle, vice-regal.

-ēakèn: See -ēacön.

-ēakêr, -ēekêr: beaker, speaker. (And extend -ēak, -ēek.)

-ēakling: meekling, treacling, weakling.

-ēakly: bleakly, meekly, sleekly, treacly, weakly, weekly; biweekly, obliquely, uniquely; semi-weekly.

-ēaky, -ēeky: beaky, bleaky, cheeky, cliquey, creaky, leaky, peeky, reeky, sheiky, sleeky, sneaky, squeaky, streaky.

-ēal: real; ideal, unreal; hymeneal. (Compare -ēal and -ēel in one-syllable rhymes.)

-ēalêr, -ēelêr: Extend -ēal and -ēel.

-ealöt: See -elàte.

-ealöus: jealous, trelliṡ, zealous; apellous, ɛn-tellus, procellous, vitellus; overzealous.

-ēalthy: healthy, stealthy, wealthy.

-ēalty: fealty, realty.

-ēaly: eely, freely, Healy, mealy, peely, really, seely, squealy, steely, wheely; genteely.

-ēamàn, -ēemàn, -ēmàn, -ēmön: beeman, demon, freeman, gleeman, G-man, he-man, leman, seaman, semen, tea-man.

-ēamêr, -ēmêr, -ēmûr: beamer, dreamer, femur, lemur, reamer, schemer, screamer, seamer, seemer, steamer, streamer, teemer; blasphemer, redeemer. (And extned -ēam.)

-ēamish: beamish, dreamish, squeamish.

-ēamstêr: See -ēemstêr.

-ēamy: beamy, creamy, dreamy, gleamy, screamy, seamy, steamy, streamy, teemy.

-ēàn, -iàn: Ian, paean; Achean, Aegean, Argean, Cadmean, Chaldean, Crimean, Judean, Korean, lethean, lyncean, nymphean, pampean, perigean, plebeian, protean; amoebean, amphigean, apogean, Caribbean, empyrean, European, Galilean, gigantean,

143

hymenean, Jacobean, Maccabean, perigean, phalangean, Tennessean; adamantean, antipodean, Archimedean, epicurean, Pythagorean.

-ēanêr, -ēanŏr: cleaner, demeanour, gleaner, greener, meaner, wiener; machiner; misdemeanor.

-ēanĕst, -ēenist, -ēnist: plenist, machinist. (Extend words under **-ean** in one-syllable rhymes for "cleanist", "obscenist", etc.)

-ēaning: gleaning, meaning. (Extend **-ēan, -ēen, -ēne, -ine.**)

-ēanō: beano, keno, Reno; Albino, bambino, casino, festino, merino, Sereno, tondino; andantino, baldachino, maraschino, peacherino, vetturino.

-ēanly: cleanly, keenly, leanly, meanly, queenly; obscenely, serenely. (And extend **-ēan.**)

-ēapêr: See **-ēap** and extend.

-ēarànce, -ērènce: clearance; adherence, appearance, arrearance, coherence, inherence; disappearance, interference, perseverance, reappearance.

-ēarêr: mirror. (Extend **-ēar, -ēre;** compare **-erà.**)

-ēarful: cheerful, earful, fearful, sneerful, tearful; uncheerful, unfearful.

144

-ēarest, -ērist: merest, querist, theorist. (And extend **-ēar**, **-ēer** and **-ēre**.)

-ēareth, -ērith: Erith. (Extend **-ēar**.)

-ēariêr, -ēeriêr, -ēriör: eerier; anterior, exterior, inferior, interior, Liberia, posterior, Siberia, superior. (And extend **-ēary̆**, **-ēery̆** for "wearier", "beerier", etc.)

-ēaring, -ēering: earring. (And extend **-ēar**, **-ēer** for "hearing", "leering", etc.)

-êarly, -îrly, -ûrly: burly, churly, curly, early, girlie, girly, pearly, Purley, Shirley, surly, swirly, twirly, whirly; hurly-burly.

-ēarly, -ēerly, -ērely: cheerly, clearly, dearly, merely, nearly, queerly, yearly; austerely, severely, sincerely; cavalierly. (Extend **-ēar**.)

-ēarment: cerement; endearment.

-ēarnĕss, -ēernĕss: sheerness. (And extend **-ēar** and **-ēer** for "clearness", "queerness", etc.)

-êarnĕst, -êrnĕst, -ûrnĕst: earnest, Ernest, furnaced, sternest, internist. (And extend words under **-êarn** for "sternest".)

-êarnêr, -êrner, -ûrner: burner, earner, learner, sojouner. (Extend **-êarn**.)

-êarning, -êrning, -ûrning: burning, earning, learning, spurning, turning, yearning; concerning, discerning, returning.

- **-ēary, -ēery, -ēry:** aerie, beery, bleary, cheery, deary, dreary, eerie, Erie, jeery, leary, peri, query, smeary, sneery, sphery, teary, veery, weary; aweary, misererc, uncheery.

- **-ēasánd, -ēasönd:** reasoned, seasoned, treasoned, weasand, wizened; unseasoned.

- **-easànt, -escènt:** crescent, peasant, pheasant, pleasant, present; decrescent, excrescent, incessant, putrescent, quiescent; convalescent, deliquescent, delitescent, effervescent, efflorescent, obsolescent, phosphorescent.

- **-ēasèl:** Diesel, easel, measle, teasel, weasel.

- **--ēasàr, -ēasèr:** beezer, Caesar, easer, freezer, friezer, geezer, greaser, leaser, pleaser, sneezer, squeezer, teaser, tweezer, wheezer; Ebenezer.

- **-ēasön:** reason, season, treason, wizen; unreason, unseason.

- **-ēastèr:** Easter, feaster; northeaster, southeaster.

- **-ēasting:** bee-sting, easting, feasting.

- **-ēastlý:** beastly, priestly.

- **-easure, -eisure:** leisure, measure, pleasure, treasure; admeasure, displeasure, entreasure, outmeasure.

- **-ēasy, -ēezy:** breezy, cheesy, easy, freezy, greasy, queasy, sleazy, sneezy, wheezy; Brin-

146

disi, speakeasy, uneasy, Zambesi.

-ēatèn, -ēetèn: Beaton, Cretan, Eaton, Eton, Keaton, Keyton. (And extend -ēat and -ēet.)

-ēatêr, -ēetêr, -ētêr, -ētre: beater, bleater, cheater, eater, fleeter, greeter, heater, liter, meeter, meter, metre, neater, Peter, praetor, seater, skeeter, sweeter, teeter, treater; beefeater, cake-eater, competer, completer, defeater, depleter, entreater, escheator, goldbeater, receipter, repeater, retreater, saltpeter, smoke-eater, unseater; centimeter, decaliter, kilometer, overeater, superheater. (Compare -ēadêr.)

-eathê, -ethêr: blether, feather, heather, Heather, leather, nether, tether, weather, wether, whether; aweather, pinfeather, together; altogether.

-ēathêr: breather, either, neither, seether, sheather, wreather.

-ēathing, -ēething: breathing, seething, sheathing, tea-thing, teething, wreathing; bequeathing.

-ēature: creature, feature. (See -ēachêr.)

-ēaty, -ēety: Beattie, meaty, peaty, sleety, sweetie, sweety, treaty; entreaty, Tahiti.

-eaty: See -etty.

-eavèn, -evèn: Bevan, Devon, Evan, heaven, leaven, Leven, seven; eleven.

-ēavèn: even, Stephen, Steven; uneven.

-ēavêr: beaver, cleaver, Eva, fever, griever, keever, leaver, lever, livre, reaver, riever, stiver, weaver, weever; achiever, believer, conceiver, deceiver, enfever, Geneva, receiver, cantilever; unbeliever. (Extend -ēve, -iēve.)

-eavy, -evy: bevy, Chevy, heavy, levee, levy, "nevvy"; top-heavy.

-ēbē: Bebe, Hebe, Phoebe, T.B.

-ebèl, -ebble: pebble, rebel, treble; arch-rebel.

-ēeble: feeble, Keble; enfeeble.

-eccā: Mecca; Rebecca. (Compare -eckêr.)

-ēcènt: decent, puissant, recent; indecent.

-echêr, -etchêr: etcher, fetcher, fletcher, lecher, retcher, sketcher, stretcher.

-echō: "dekko", echo, gecko, secco; El Greco, re-echo.

-ēcian, -ētion: Grecian, accretion, completion, concretion, deletion, depletion, excretion, impletion, Phoenician, repletion, secretion, Venetian; incompletion, internecion.

-ēciès: Decies, species. (Add "s" to -ēace; thus "fleeces", "ceases", "mantelpieces", etc.)

-ēcious: specious; facetious.

-eckêr, -equêr: "brekker", checker, chequer,

decker, flecker, pecker, trekker, wrecker;
bedecker, exchequer, henpecker, woodpeck-
er. (And extend -eck and -eque. Compare
-ecca.)

-eckle, -ekel: deckle, freckle, heckle, keckle,
Seckel, shekel, speckle; bespeckle; Dr.
Jekyll.

-eckless, -ecklace: feckless, fleckless, necklace,
reckless, speckless.

-eckon: beckon, reckon. (Preterites of same
rhyme with "second" and "fecund".)

-ectant: expectant, reflectent; disinfectant.

-ectful: neglectful, respectful; disrespectful.

-ectic: hectic, pectic; eclectic, electric; ana-
lectic, apoplectic, catalectic, dialectic.

-ection, -exion: flection, lection, section; affec-
tion, bisection, collection, complexion, con-
fection, connection, convection, correction,
defection, deflection, dejection, detection,
direction, dissection, ejection, election, erec-
tion, infection, inflection, injection, inspec-
tion, objection, perfection, projection, pro-
tection, reflection, rejection, selection, sub-
jection, subsection; circumspection, disaf-
fection, disinfection, imperfection, indirec-
tion, insurrection, interjection, introspec-
tion, misdirection, recollection, resurrection,
vivisection.

-ective: sective; affective, collective, connective, corrective, defective, deflective, detective, directive, effective, elective, erective, infective, inflective, injective, inspective, invective, neglective, objective, perfective, perspective, prospective, protective, refective, reflective, rejective, respective, selective, subjective; circumspective, ineffective, introspective, irrespective, recollective, retrospective.

-ectör, -ectre: flector, hector, Hector, lector, nectar, rector, sector, specter, vector; collector, deflector, detector, director, ejecter, elector, injecter, inspector, objector, prospector, protector, reflector, selector.

-ecture: lecture; confecture, conjecture, prefecture, projecture; architecture.

-edàl, -eddle, -edule: heddle, medal, meddle, pedal, peddle, reddle, schedule, treadle; intermeddle. (Compare -ettle.)

-ēdàr: cedar. (And extend -ēad.)

-eddar: Cheddar. (See -ettêr.)

-eddy, -eady: eddy, Freddy, heady, Neddy, ready, shreddy, steady, Teddy; already, unready, unsteady.

-ēdéd: Extend -ēad. (Compare -ēatéd.)

-ēdèn: Eden, Sweden. (Compare -ēatén.)

150

-ēdéd: Extend -ead. (Compare -ēated.)

-ēdénce: credence, precedence; antecedence, intercedence.

-ēdént: credent, needn't, sedent; decedent, precedent; antecedent, intercedent, retrocedent.

-ēdêr: See -ēadêr.

-edgêr: edger, dredger, hedger, ledger, pledger, sledger, spedger, wedger.

-edgewâre: Edgeware, sledge-wear.

-edit: credit, edit; accredit, discredit, miscredit, sub-edit.

-ēdium: medium, tedium.

-edlàr: medlar, meddler, peddler, pedlar, treadler. (Extend -edàl. Compare -ettle.)

-ēedléss: Extend -ēad; compare -ēat.

-edleẏ, eadlẏ: deadly, medley, redly, Sedley.

-ēdō: credo, Lido; libido, stampedo, teredo, toledo, Toledo, torpedo, tuxedo.

-ēechy, -ēachy: Extend -ēach and -ēech.

-ēecy: fleecy, greasy.

-ēedle: See -ēadle.

-ēedẏ: beady, creedy, deedy, greedy, heedy, Leedy, needy, reedy, seedy, speedy, weedy; indeedy, unheedy.

-ēelẏ: See -ēalẏ.

151

-ēefy: beefy, leafy, reefy, sheafy.

-ēemstêr: deemster, seamster, teamster.

-ēenish, -ēanish: Extend -ēan and -ēen in one-syllable rhymes.

-ēeny, -ēnē: Cheney, Sheyney, genie, greeny, meanie, meany, Selene, sheeny, spleeny, Sweeney, teeny, visne, weeny; Athene, bikini, Cellini, Houdini, martini, Puccini; Mussolini.

-ēepèn: cheapen, deepen, steepen.

-ēeper: cheaper, creeper, deeper, keeper, leaper, peeper, reaper, sleeper, steeper, sweeper. (Extend -ēap.)

-ēepiêr: creepier, sleepier.

-ēeple, -ēople: people, steeple; unpeople.

-ēeply: cheaply, deeply. (Extend -ēep.)

-ēerage: beerage, clearage, peerage, pierage, steerage; arrearage.

-ēerful: See -ēarful.

-ēery: See -ēary.

-ēestōne: freestone, keystone; sea-stone.

-ēesy: See -ēasy.

-ēetèn: See -ēatèn.

-ēetêr: See -ēatêr.

-ēetle: beetle, betel, fetal; decretal.

-ēety: See -ēaty.

-ēevish, -iēvish: peevish, thievish.

-ēezêr: See -ēasár.

-efty: hefty, lefty, wefty.

-ēgàl: See -ēagle.

-eggàr, -eggêr: beggar, dregger, egger, kegger, pegger; bootlegger.

-eggy: dreggy, eggy, leggy, Meggie, Peggy.

-ēgian, -ēgion: Fijian, kegion, legion, region; collegian, Glaswegian, Norwegian.

-egnànt: pregnant, regnant; impregnant.

-ēgrèss: egress, Negress, regress.

-ēgret: egret, regret.

-eifêr: See eaf-êr.

-eighbör: See -ābör.

-eighty: See -āty.

-ēiling: ceiling. (Extend -ēel, -ēal.)

-eirèss (āir): heiress; mayoress.

-ēist: deist, beest, fleest, freest, seest, theist.

-ēithêr: See -ēathêr.

-eīthêr: See -īthêr.

-ēivêr: See -ēavêr.

-elàte, -elöt: helot, pellet, prelate, stellate, zealot; appellate, constellate; interpellate.

-eldàm, -eldöm: beldam, seldom.

-eldêr: elder, gelder, melder, welder.

-elding: gelding, welding.

-elfish: elfish, selfish, shell-fish.

-elic: bellic, melic, relic, telic; angelic, nick-elic, parhelic, Pentelic, pimelic; archangelic, evangelic.

-ēline: beeline, feline, sea-line.

-elish, -ellish: hellish, relish; embellish.

-ellá: Bella, Ella, Lella, Stella; capella, Lou-ella, patella, prunella, umbrella; **Arabella,** Cinderella, Isabella, tarantella. (**Compare -ellêr.**)

-ellêr: cellar, dweller, feller, heller, seller, smeller, speller, stellar, teller; impeller, pro-peller, saltcellar; fortune teller.

-ellis: trellis. (See **-ealous.**)

-ellist, -ellised: trellised, 'cellist. (And extend **-ell** for "dwellest", etc.)

-ellō, -ellōe, -ellōw: bellow, 'cello, felloe, fel-low, hello, Jello, mellow, yellow; duello, good-fellow, Martello, morello, niello, pru-nello; Portobello, Punchinello; violoncello.

-elly: belly, Delhi, felly, helly, jelly, Kelly, Nelly, Shelley, shelly, smelly; cancelli; **Dona-telli,** vermicelli.

-elön: felon, melon.

-elpêr: Belper, helper, yelper.

-elsiē: Elsie, Chelsea, Selsey.

154

-eltêr: belter, felter, helter, kelter, melter, pelter, shelter, skelter, smelter, spelter, svelter, swelter, welter.

-embêr: ember, member; December, dismember, November, remember, September; disremember.

-emble: Kemble, semble, tremble; assemble, dissemble, resemble; reassemble.

-embly̆: trembly, Wembley; assembly.

-emi, -emmy: clemmy, demi, hemi, Jemmy.

-ēmiêr, -ēamiêr: creamier, dreamier, steamier.

-emisĕs: nemesis, premises.

-emic: chemic; alchemic, endemic, pandemic, polemic, systemic, totemic; academic, epidemic, theoremic; stratagemic.

-emish: blemish, Flemish; unblemish.

-emist: chemist, hemmest, premised, stemmest.

-ēmist: extremest. (Extend -ēam, -ēme.)

-emlin: gremlin, Kremlin.

-emmȧ: Emma, gemma; dilemma.

-emŏr: hemmer, tremor; condemner, contemner.

-emplȧr: templar; exemplar.

-emptêr: tempter; attempter, exempter, preemptor, unkempter.

155

-emption: emption; ademption, co-emption, diremption, exemption, pre-emption, redemption.

-ēmū: emu, seamew.

-ēmûr: See **-ēamêr.**

-ēmüse: bemuse, emus, seamews.

-ēná: Ena, Gena, Lena, Nina, scena, Tina, Zena; arena, Athena, catena, farina, Galena, hyena, Medina, Modena, patina, Serena, Tsarina; Argentina, concertina, Pasadena, scarlatina, semolina, signorina, Wilhelmina. (Compare **-ēanêr, -ēanör.**)

-enáce, -ennis, -ennous: Dennis, menace, pennous, tenace, tennis, Venice; impennous, vaginopennous.

-ēnâl: penal, renal, venal; adrenal, machinal; duodenal.

-enant: pennant, tenant; lieutenant.

-enáte: See **-ennêt.**

-encêr: See **-ensêr.**

-encefôrth: henceforth, thenceforth.

-encêr: See **-ensêr.**

-enchêr, -ensure, -entûre: bencher, blencher, clencher, drencher, quencher, trencher, wrencher; adventure, bedrencher, debenture, indenture; misadventure, preadventure. (Extend **-ench.**)

-encil, -ensàl: mensal, pencil, pensil, pensile, stencil, tensile; extensile, prehensile, utensil.

-endà: Brenda, Zenda; agenda, delenda; corrigenda, hacienda. (Compare -endêr.)

-endànt, -endént: pendant, pendent; appendant, ascendant, attendant, contendant, defendant, dependant, dependent, descendant, descendent, impendent, intendant, resplendent, transcendent, transplendent; equipendent, interdependent, superintendent.

-endêr, -endör: bender, blender, ender, fender, gender, lender, mender, render, sender, slender, spender, splendor, tender, vendor, wender; amender, ascender, attender, commender, contender, defender, depender, descender, emender, engender, expender, extender, intender, offender, pretender, surrender, suspender; apprehender, comprehender, money-lender, recommender, reprehender.

-endön: Hendon, tendon.

-endous: horrendous, stupendous, tremendous.

-endum: addendum, agendum, credendum; corrigendum, referendum.

-ènglish: English, jinglish, tinglish.

-engthèn: lengthen, strengthen.

-ēniàl: genial, menial, venial; congenial.

-enic: phrenic, scenic, splenic; arsenic (adj.),

eugenic, Hellenic, irenic, lichenic, parthenic, selenic; callisthenic, diplogenic, neurasthenic, oxygenic, paragenic, pathogenic, photogenic, protogenic, pyrogenic, telegenic.

-enin: Benin, Lenin, Menin.

-ēniôr: senior, senor, signor; teenier, weenier.

-enish: plenish, rhenish, tenish, wennish; replenish.

-ēnist: See -ēanést.

-ennà: henna, senna; antenna, duenna, Gehenna, Ravenna, Siena, sienna, Vienna.

-ennèl: fennel, kennel, phenyl; antennal.

-ennêr, -enör: penner, tenor. (And extend -en.)

-ennèt, -enàte: Bennett, jennet, kennet, rennet, senate, tenet.

-ennis: See -enàce.

-ennön, -enön: pennon, tenon.

-enny, -any: any, Benny, Denny, fenny, jenny, Jenny, Kenny, Lenny, many, penny, tenny, wenny; Kilkenny, Albergavenny.

-ensêr, -ensör, -encêr: censer, censor, Spencer. (Extend -ence, -ense.)

-ensive: pensive, tensive; ascensive, defensive, descensive, distensive, expensive, extensive, offensive, ostensive, protensive, suspensive; apprehensive, comprehensive, inexpensive, recompensive, reprehensive, self-defensive.

-ension: See **-entian.**

-entàl, -entil, -entle: cental, dental, dentil, dentile, gentle, Lental, mental, rental, trental; fragmental, parental, placental, segmental, tridental, ungentle; accidental, argumental, complemental, continental, departmental, detrimental, documental, elemental, fundamental, governmental, incidental, instrumental, monumental, occidental, oriental, ornamental, parliamental, regimental, rudimental, sacramental, sentimental, supplemental, testamental, transcendental.

-entànce, -entènce: sentence, repentance.

-entêr, -entôr: centaur, center, enter, lentor, mentor, renter, tenter; dissenter, frequenter, inventor, lamenter, off-center, precentor, re-enter, repenter, tormentor; ornamenter; experimenter.

-entian, -ention, -ension: gentian, mention, pension, tension; abstention, ascension, ascention, attention, contention, convention, declension, detension, dimension, dissension, distension, extension, intension, intention, invention, prehension, pretension, prevention, propension, subvention, suspension; apprehension, circumvention, comprehension, condescension, intervention, reprehension, supervention.

-entice, -entis: pentice, prentice, apprentice;

compos mentis.

-entīle: Gentile, pentile; percentile.

-entist, -entèst, -enticed: dentist; Adventist, apprenticed, preventist. (And extend **-ent.**)

-entle, -entil: See **-entàl.**

-entràl: central, ventral.

-entrỳ: entry, gentry, sentry, comment'ry, invent'ry; element'ry, parliament'ry.

-enture: See **-enchêr.**

-enty: plenty, scenty, twenty; festina lente, dolce far niente.

-enū: menu, venue.

-ēnus: genus, Venus.

-ēō: Cleo, Leo, Rio, trio, yeo.

-ēōle: creole, key-hole.

-ēon: aeon, Creon, Fijian, Leon, neon, peon, pheon, pantheon, plebeian; Anacreon.

-eopárd, -ephêrd, -eppêred: jeopard, leopard, peppered, shepherd.

-epid: tepid, trepid; intrepid.

-ephỳr: deafer, heifer, zephyr. (See **-eafêr.**)

-ēpŏt (pō): Beppo, depot: Aleppo.

-eppêr, -epêr: leper, pepper, stepper; high-stepper.

-epping: Epping, stepping.

-eppy: peppy, Sheppey.

-eptic: peptic, sceptic, septic, skeptic; aseptic, dispeptic, enpeptic, eupeptic; antiseptic, cataleptic, epileptic.

-eptör: sceptre; accepter, adepter, excepter, inceptor, preceptor, susceptor; intercepter.

-ēquàl, -ēquèl: equal, sequel; co-equal, unequal.

-ēquénce: frequence, sequence.

-erà: era, Hera, lira, Vera; chimera, Madeira. (Compare -ēarêr, -errör.)

-eràld: Gerald, ferruled, herald; imperilled.

-êrbàl, -ûrble: burble, herbal, verbal.

-êrcêr, -êrsêr, -ûrsàr: bursar, cursor, mercer, nurser, purser; disburser, precursor. (And extend -êrse for "terser", etc.)

-êrcy, -ûrsy: Circe, mercy, nursey, Percy, pursy; grammercy; controversy.

-êrdêr: Extend -êrd; compare -êrtêr, -îrdêr.

-ēréàl, -ēriàl: cereal, ferial, serial, arterial, ethereal, funereal, imperial, material, venereal; immaterial, ministerial.

-ērést: severest. (See -ēarést.)

-êrgency: emergency, urgency.

-èrgent: convergent, detergent, divergent, emergent, resurgent, urgent.

-êrgêr, -êrdure, -ûrger: merger, perjure, purger, scourger, urger, verdure, verger; deterger, converger, diverger, emergcr; submerger.

-êrgénce: convergence, divergence, emergence, resurgence, submergence.

-erét: See -erit.

-êrgy, -îrgy, -ûrgy: clergy, dirgy, sergy, surgy; liturgy; dramaturgy, metallurgy.

-eric, -errick: Berwick, cleric, Derek, derrick, Eric, ferric, Herrick, Lerwick, spheric; chimeric, enteric, generic, Homeric, hysteric, mesmeric, numeric, suberic, valeric; atmospheric, Chromospheric, esoteric, exoteric, hemispheric, peripheric.

-eril, -errule, -erÿl: beryl, Beryl, Errol, ferrule, imperil, peril, spherule, sterile.

-erish: cherish, perish.

-erit. -errét: ferret, merit; demerit, inherit; disinherit.

-êrjûre: See -êrgêr.

-êrkin: firkin, gherkin, jerkin, merkin, Perkin.

-êrky, -ûrky: jerky, murky, perky, smirky, turkey, Turkey.

-êrling: See -îrling.

-ermàl: dermal, thermal.

162

-êrmán, -êrmön: Burman, Firman, German, Herman, merman, sermon; Omdurman.

-êrment: ferment; affirmant, averment, bestirment, deferment, determent, interment, preferment, referment; disinterment.

-êrmin, -êrmine: ermine, vermin; determine, predetermine. (See -êrmán.)

-êrmit: hermit, Kermit, permit (noun).

-êrmy̆: fermi, squirmy, wormy; diathermy, taxidermy.

-êrnál, -êrnél, -olonél, -oûrnál, -ûrnál: colonel, journal, kernel, sternal, urnal, vernal; cavernal, diurnal, eternal, external, fraternal, hibernal, infernal, internal, lucernal, maternal, nocturnal, paternal, supernal; coeternal, hodiernal, sempiternal.

-êrnárd: Bernard, gurnard.

-ērō: hero, Nero, pierrot, zero.

-erránd: errand, gerund.

-erriêr: burier, ferrier, merrier, terrier.

-êring: derring, erring, herring.

-errör: error, parer, terror. (Extend -âir, āre; compare -erā.)

-errule: See -eril.

-erry: berry, bury, Bury, cherry, Derry, ferry, Jerry, Kerry, merry, Perry, sherry, skerry, Terry, very, wherry; Bambury, blackberry,

163

blueberry, cranberry, gooseberry, mulberry, raspberry, strawberry; beriberi, cemetery, lamasery, millinery, monastery, presbytery, stationary, stationery. (Compare -àrỳ.)

-êrseỳ, -ûrzỳ: furzy, jersey, Jersey, kersey, Mersey; New Jersey.

-êrsion, -êrtian, -êrtion, -ûrsion: mersion, Persian, tertian, version; absterstion, aspersion, assertion, aversion, coercion, conversion, demersion, desertion, detersion, discursion, dispersion, diversion, emersion, excursion, exertion, immersion, incursion, insertion, inversion, perversion, recursion, reversion, submersion, subversion; extroversion, introversion; animadversion.

-êrsön, -ôrsèn: person, worsen; McPherson.

-êrsus: thyrsus, versus.

-êrtain, -ûrtain: Burton, certain, curtain, Gerton, Merton; uncertain.

-êrtêr: blurter, curter, flirter, hurter, squirter; asserter, averter, converter, deserter, diverter, exerter, inserter, inverter, perverter, subverter. (Extend -êrt, -îrt, -ûrt. See -êrdêr, -îrtêr.)

-êrtèst: Extend -êrt, -îrt, -ûrt.

-êrtile: See -îrtle. (Compare -îrdle.)

-êrtion: See -îrsion.

-êrtly: curtly, pertly; alertly, expertly, inertly, invertly, overtly; inexpertly.

-êrvánt, -êrvènt: curvant, fervent, servant ; conservant, observant, recurvant; unobservant.

-êrvêr, -êrvör: fervor, nerver, server, swerver; conserver, observer, preserver, reserver, timeserver.

-êrvid: fervid, perfervid, scurvied. (And accentuate "-ed" on -êrve, -úrve.)

-êrvish: curvish, dervish, nervish, swervish.

-êrvy, -úrvy: curvy, nervy, scurvy; topsy-turvy.

-ēry: See -ēary.

-eságe, -esságe: dressage, message, presage; expressage.

-escénce, -essénce: essence; excrescence, florescence, pubescence, putrescence, quiescence, quintessence, senescence, turgescence, vitrescence; adolescence, coalescence, convalescence, deliquescence, delitescence, effervescence, efflorescence, evanescence, inflorescence, incalescence, incandescence, iridescence, obsolescence, phosphorescence, recrudescence, revalescence, revirescence, virilescence.

-escience: nescience, prescience.

-escént: cessant, crescent, jessant; accrescent, depressant, excrescent, fluorescent, incessant,

165

increscent, liquescent, putrescent, quiescent, rubescent, senescent, virescent, vitrescent; adolescent, coalescent, convalescent, deliquescent, effervescent, incandescent, obsolescent, opalescent, phosphorescent, recrudescent, superscrescent. (See -aasént.)

-escō: fresco, Tresco; alfresco.

-escū: fescue, rescue; Montesquieu.

-esénce, -easánce: pleasance, presence; omnipresence. (Extend -easánt as in "pheasants".)

-eshêr: fresher, pressure, thresher; refresher.

-eshly: fleshly, freshly; unfleshly.

-esion: session, concession, discretion, secession. (And extend -ess for "profession", etc.)

-ēsion: lesion; adhesion, artesian, cohesion, Ephesioan, inhesion, magnesion, Parisian, Silesian; Indonesian, Polynesian.

-ēsis: thesis; anthesis, deesis, diesis, mimesis; catachresis, exegesis, synteresis; hyperesthesis. (And extend certain words under -ēace for "ceases", etc.)

-esságe: See -eságe.

-essál: See -estle.

-essénce: See -escénce.

-essêr, -essôr: dresser, guesser, lesser, lessor,

166

messer, presser; addresser, aggressor, asses-
sor, compressor, confessor, depressor, opres-
sor, possessor, professor, successor, sup-
pressor, transgressor; antecessor, interces-
or, predecessor, second-guesser.

-essure: pressure. (And extend **-esh** for "flesh-
er", "refresher", etc.)

-essy: Bessie, Crecy, dressy, Jessie, messy,
Tessie, tressy.

-estàl, -estle: festal, pestle, vestal.

-estèd: rested, vested. (Extend **-est.**)

-estêr: Chester, Ester, Esther, fester, Hester,
jester, Leicester, Lester, Nestor, pester,
tester, vester, wrester; digester, investor,
Manchester, molester, protester, semester,
sequester, Sylvester, trimester, Westchester;
midsemester. (Extend **-est.**)

-estial: bestial; celestial.

-estic: gestic; agrestic, asbestic, majestic,
telestic; anapestic, catachrestic.

-estige: prestige, vestige.

-estine: destine; clandestine, intestine, pre-
destine.

-estive: estive, festive, restive; attestive, con-
gestive, digestive, infestive, investive, sug-
gestive, tempestive.

-estle (silent "t"): Cecil, Chessel, nestle, pestle, trestle, vessel, wrestle; redressal, unnestle.

-esto: presto; manifesto.

-estral, estrel: kestrel, ancestral, fenestral, orchestral, trimestral.

-estûre: gesture, vesture; divesture, investure.

-esty: chesty, cresty, pesty, resty, testy.

-ētāil: detail, retail.

-etăl: See -ettle.

-etchêr: See -echêr.

-etchy: fetchy, sketchy, stretchy, tetchy.

-ētely: fleetly, meetly, neatly, sweetly; completely, concretely, discreetly, unmeetly; incompletely, indiscreetly, obsoletely.

-etful: fretful, forgetful, regretful.

-ethèl: Bethel, Ethel, ethyl, methyl.

-ethêr: See -eathêr.

-etic: aesthetic, ascetic, athletic, bathetic, colletic, cosmetic, docetic, emetic, frenetic, genetic, hermetic, kinetic, magnetic, paretic, pathetic, phonetic, phrenetic, poetic, prophetic, splenetic, syncretic, synthetic, theoretic; alphabetic, amuletic, anesthetic, anchoretic, antithetic, apathetic, arithmetic, catechetic, dietetic, energetic, epithetic, eugenetic, hypothetic, pangenetic, para-

168

thetic, parenthetic, strategetic, sympathetic,
theoretic; antipathetic, apologetic, biomag-
netic, diamagnetic, diaphoretic, homoge-
netic, logarithmetic, pathogenetic, peripa-
tetic; abiogenetic, idiopathic; onomato-
poetic.

-ētion: See -ēcian.

-ētör, -ētêr: See -ēater.

-ettêr, -ettör: better, bettor, debtor, fetter,
getter, letter, setter, wetter, whetter; abet-
tor, begetter, forgetter, go-getter, typeset-
ter, unfetter.

-ettish, -etish: fetish, Lettish, pettish, wet-
tish; coquettish.

-ettle, -etàl: fettle, Gretel, kettle, metal, met-
tle, nettle, petal, settle; abettal, unsettle.
(Compare -edàl, -eddle.)

-ettō: ghetto, petto; falsetto, libretto, palmet-
to, stiletto, terzetto, zucchetto; allegretto,
amoretto, lazaretto, Rigoletto.

-etty, -eti, -etti: betty, Betty, fretty, Hettie,
Hetty, jetty, Letty, netty, petti, petty,
sweaty; confetti, libretti, Rosetti, spaghetti;
spermacetti, Vanizetti. (See -eddy.)

-ētus: Cletus, fetus; acetous, quietus.

-eūdàl: See -ōōdle.

-eūtêr: See -ōōtêr.

-evél: bevel, devil, Greville, level, Neville,

169

revel; bedevil, dishevel.

-evèn: See -eavèn.

-ēvèn: See -ēavèn.

-evêr: clever, ever, lever, never, sever, Trevor; assever, dissever, endeavor, however, whatever, whenever, wherever, whichever, whomever, whoever; howsoever, whatsoever, whensoever, wheresoever, whomsoever, whosoever.

-ēvêr: See -ēavêr.

-evêrèst: Everest, cleverest.

-ēvil: evil, weevil; coeval, primeval, retrieval, upheaval; medieval.

-evil: See -evèl.

-ēvious: devious, previous.

-evy: See -eavy.

-ewàge: brewage, "New Age", sewage; escuage.

-ewàrd, -ewêred: leeward, Seward, sewered, secured, skewered, steward.

-ewèl, -ūél: crewel, cruel, dual, duel, Ewell, fuel, gruel, jewel, newel, ruelle; bejewel, eschewal, pursual, renewal, reviewal, subdual. (Compare -ōōl and -ūle.)

-ewêr: bluer, booer, grewer, chewer, Clewer, cooer, doer, fewer, hewer, newer, screwer, sewer, skewer, strewer, truer, twoer, view-

170

er, wooer; construer, pursuer, renewer, reviewer; interviewer.

-ewèss: Jewess, Lewis, Louis, U.S., St. Louis.

-ewish: blueish, Jewish, newish, shrewish, truish, twoish.

-ewtêr, -eūtêr, -ūtêr, -ūtör: cuter, hooter, looter, mooter, muter, neuter, pewter, rooter, scooter, suitor, tutor; commuter, computer, disputer, freebooter, polluter, refuter.

-ewy, -ouė, -ūey: bluey, chewy, coo-ee, Coue, dewy, fluey, gluey, gooey, hooey, Louie, Louis, pfui, roue, screwy, thewy; viewy; chop suey.

-exīle: exile, flexile.

-exôr, -exêr: flexor, vexer; annexer, perplexer.

-exion: See **-ection.**

-extànt: extant, sextant.

-extīle: sextile, textile.

-exus: nexus, plexus; Texas; Alexis.

-exy: prexy, sexy; apoplexy.

-eyànce: seance; abeyance, conveyance, purveyance.

-eyör: See **-āyêr.**

-ïad: dryad, dyad, naiad, triad; hamadryad, jeremiad.

-ïàl, -ïöl: dial, Dyall, phial, Lyell, trial, vial,

171

viol; decrial, denial, espial, retrial, sundial, supplial. (Compare -ile in one-syllable list.)

-iàn: See **-ëön.**

-iànce, -iènce: clients, giants, science; affiance, alliance, appliance, compliance, defiance, reliance, suppliance; misalliance.

-iànt, -iènt: Bryant, client, giant, pliant, scient; affiant, compliant, defiant, reliant; self-reliant.

-iär: briar, brier, buyer, drier, Dwyer, dyer, flier, friar, fryer, higher, liar, mire, nigher, plier, prior, pryer, shyer, sigher, slyer, spryer, spyer, tire, trier, Tyre, vier. (Extend -y. Compare -ire.)

-iàs: bias, pious; Elias, Tobias; Ananias, nisi-prius.

-iàt, -ièt, -iöt: diet, fiat, quiet, riot, ryot, striate, Wyatt; disquiet.

-ibàld: ribald. (Extend -ibble for "quibbled", etc.)

-ibbêr: bibber, cribber, dibber, fibber, gibber, glibber, jibber, nibber, quibber, squibber; wine-bibber.

-ibbèt, -ibit: gibbet, Tibbett; cohibit, exhibit, inhibit, prohibit.

-ibble: cribble, dibble, dribble, fribble, gribble, kibble, nibble, quibble, Ribble, scribble, Sybil, thribble; ish ka bibble.

172

-ibbling: Extend **-ibble.**

-ibbly: dribbly, fribbly, glibly, nibbly, quibbly, scribbly, tribbly.

-ibbon: gibbon, ribbon.

-ībêr: briber, fiber, giber, Khyber, Tiber; ascriber, imbiber, inscriber, prescriber, subscriber, transcriber.

-īble, -ībàl: Bible, liable, libel, tribal.

-iblét: driblet, giblet, triblet.

-icàr, -ickêr: bicker, clicker, dicker, flicker, kicker, knicker, licker, liquor, nicker, picker, pricker, quicker, sicker, slicker, snicker, sticker, thicker, ticker, tricker, vicar, wicker.

-ichês, -itchês: breeches, riches. (And extend **-itch.**)

-ician, -icion, -ition, -ission: fission, mission; addition, admisson, ambition, attrition, audition, cognition, coition, commission, condition, contrition, edition, emission, fruition, Galician, ignition, insition, logician, magician, nutrition, omission, optician, partition, patrician, perdition, permission, petition, physician, position, prodition, reddition, remission, rendition, sedition, submission, suspicion, transition, transmission, tuition, volition; ammunition, apparition, apposition, circuition, circumcision, coali-

173

tion, competition, composition, definition, demolition, deposition, disparition, disquisition, ebullition, electrician, emolition, erudition, exhibition, expedition, exposition, imposition, inanition, inhibition, inquisition, intermission, intromission, intuition, opposition, parturition, politician, precognition, premonition, preposition, preterition, prohibition, proposition, readmission, recognition, recommission, repetition, reposition, requisition, rhetorician, superstition, supposition, transposition; arithmetician, contraposition, decomposition, geometrician, indisposition, interposition, juxtaposition, mathematician, metaphysician, predisposition, presupposition, recomposition.

-icious, -itious: vicious; ambitious, auspicious, capricious, cilicious, delicious, factitious, fictitious, flagitious, ignitious, judicious, malicious, Mauritius, nutritious, officious, pernicious, propitious, seditious, suspicious; adventitious, avaricious, expeditious, inauspicious, injudicious, meretricious, superstitious, supposititious, surrepititious.

-ickėn: chicken, quicken, sicken, stricken, thicken, wicken.

-ickêr: See -icàr.

-ickét: clicket, cricket, picket, piquet,, pricket, snicket, spicate, thicket, ticket, wicket; in-

174

tricate.

-ickle, -ickel: chicle, fickle, mickle, nickel, pickle, prickle, sickle, stickle, strickle, tickle, trickle. (See **-ycle.**)

-ickly: prickley, quickly, sickly, slickly, thickly, trickly.

-ickshaw: kickshaw, rickshaw.

-icky: bricky, dickey, Dickey, Ficke, Mickey, Nickey, quickie, rickey, sticky, thicky, tricky, Vicki; doohickey, Kon-tiki.

-ictêr, -ictör: lictor, stricter, victor, Victor; afflicter, conflicter, constrictor, inflicter, predicter; contradicter; boa constrictor.

-iction, -ixion: diction, fiction, friction; addiction, adstriction, affliction, affixion, affriction, astriction, confliction, constriction, conviction, depiction, eviction, indiction, infliction, abstriction, prediction, prefixion, reliction, restriction, reviction, transfixion; benediction, contradiction, dereliction, interdiction, jurisdiction, malediction, valediction.

-ictive: fictive; addictive, afflictive, conflictive, constrictive, convictive, depictive, indictive, inflictive, predictive, restrictive, vindictive; benedictive, contradictive, interdictive, jurisdictive.

-icture: picture, stricture; depicture.

-ictus: ictus; Benedictus, acronyctous.

-icy: icy, spicy.

-idàl, -īdle, -idöl: bridal, bridle, idle, idol, idyll, sidle, tidal; fratricidal, homicidal, matricidal, parricidal, regicidal, suicidal; infanticidal, tyrannicidal.

-idày: See **-idy**.

-iddèn: bidden, chidden, hidden, midden, ridden, slidden, stridden; forbidden, unbidden.

-idder: bidder, kidder. (Compare **-itter**.)

-iddish: kiddish, Yiddish.

-iddle: diddle, fiddle, griddle, middle, piddle, quiddle, riddle, tiddle, twiddle. (See **-ittle**.)

-iddling: Extend **-iddle**. See **-ittle**.

-iddy: Biddy, giddy, kiddie, middy, skiddy, stiddy.

-īdè: See **-īdy**.

-īdèn, -īdön: guidon, Haydn, Leyden, Sidon, widen.

-īdènt: bident, guidant, rident, strident, trident; dividant.

-idèous: hideous; fastidious, insidious, invidious, lapidious, perfidious.

-īdêr: cider, eider, glider, guider, hider, rider, spider, wider; backslider, confider, divider, insider, outrider, provider.

-idgèt, -igit: Bridget, digit, fidget, midget.

-idgy: midgy, ridgy.

-īdle: See -īdäl.

-īdly, -īdely: idly, widely.

-idnēy: kidney, Sidney.

-īdẏ: Friday, sidy, tidy; untidy; bona fide.

-iēflẏ: briefly, chiefly.

-iēnce: See -īänce.

-iēnt: See -īänt.

-iêr: See -iär.

-iēst, -īghèst: Extend -y, -īgh; also "biassed."

-iēstly: See -ēastly.

-iēt: See -īät.

-iēvêr: See -ēavêr.

-īfêr, -īphêr: cipher, fifer, knifer, lifer, rifer; decipher.

-iffêr: biffer, differ, sniffer.

-iffin: Biffen, biffin, griffin, griffon, stiffen, tiffin.

-iffle: piffle, riffle, sniffle, whifflle.

-iffy: jiffy, Liffy, niffy, sniffy, spiffy, squiffy, whiffy.

-ific: glyphic; deific, grandific, horrific, magnific, pacific, pontific, prolific, pulsific, rubific, sacrific, sensific, somnific, specific, tabific, terrific, vivific; beatific, anaglyphic, calorific, colorific, dolorific, hieroglyphic,

177

honorific, humorific, lapidific, photoglyphic, saporific, scientific, sonorific, soporific.

-ifle: Eiffel, eyeful, rifle, stifle, trifle.

-ifling: rifling, stifling, trifling.

-iftêr: drifter, grifter, lifter, shifter, sifter, snifter, swifter, shop-lifter, uplifter.

-iftlèss: driftless, shiftless, thriftless.

-ifty: clifty, drifty, fifty, "giftie", nifty, rifty, shifty, thrifty.

-igàte: See **-igöt.**

-igeön, -idgeön: pigeon, Phrygian, Stygian, widgeon ; religion; irreligion.

-īgêr: Niger, tiger.

-īgest: digest (noun); obligest.

-iggêr, -igôr: bigger, chigger, digger, figger, jigger, nigger, rigger, rigor, snigger, swigger, trigger, twigger, vigor; configure, disfigure, gold digger, grave digger, outrigger, transfigure.

-iggêred: figgered, jiggered, niggard.

-iggin: biggin, piggin.

-iggish: riggish. (And extended **-ig.**)

-iggle: giggle, higgle, jiggle, niggle, sniggle, squiggle, wiggle, wriggle.

-igly, iggly: bigly, giggly, sniggly, wriggly; piggly-wiggly.

-iggy: iggy, piggy, twiggy.

-īghêr: See -īār.

-īghländ: highland, island.

-īghly: See -īly.

-īghtën, -ītën: brighten, Brighton, Crichtin, frighten, heighten, lighten, tighten, Titan, whiten; enlighten. (And extend -īte and īght.)

-īghtêr, -ītêr: biter, blighter, brighter, citer, fighter, flighter, lighter, miter, niter, plighter, righter, sighter, slighter, smiter, tighter, triter, whiter, writer; alighter, exciter, igniter, inciter, indicter, inviter, moonlighter, politer, typewriter, uniter; copywriter, dynamiter, underwriter.

-īghtful: frightful, mightful, rightful, spiteful, sprightful; delightful.

-īghtly: brightly, knightly, lightly, nightly, rightly, sightly, slightly, sprightly, tightly, tritely, whiteley, whitely; politely, unknightly, unsightly, uprightly.

-īghtning: brightening, frightening, lightning, tightening, whitening.

-īghty: Blighty, Clytie, flighty, mighty, nightie, whitey, almighty, Aphrodite.

-igil: sigil, strigil, vigil.

-igmä: sigma, stigma, enigma.

-igmënt: figment, pigment.

-igöt, -igàte: bigot, frigate, gigot, spigot.

-igûr: See -iggêr.

-igress: digress, tigress.

-īkèn, -īcön: Dicon, icon, lichen, liken.

-īking: biking, dyking, piking, spiking, striking, viking; well-liking.

-īky: Ikey, crikey, Psyche, spiky.

-īlacs, īlax: lilacs, smilax.

-ilbêrt: filbert, Gilbert, Wilbert.

-ildêr: builder, gilder, guilder, Hilda; bewilder, Matilda, St. Kilda.

-īldêr: milder, wilder.

-īldish: childish, mildish, wildish.

-īldly: childly, mildly, wildly.

-ilè: See -illy.

-ilful: skillful, wilful; unskillful.

-īlīght: dry-light, highlight, skylight, twilight, Xylite.

-īling: filing, piling, riling, smiling, styling, tiling, whiling, wiling; beguiling, compiling, defiling, reviling, up-piling.

-īlkèn: milken, silken.

-ilky: milky, silky, Willkie.

-illà: Scylla, villa; anilla, armilla, barilla, cedilla, chinchilla, codilla, gorilla, guerrilla, Manila, mantilla, maxilla, Priscilla, Sybilla, vanilla; camarilla, cassarilla, granadilla, sabadilla, sapodilla, seguidilla.

-illáge: billage, grillage, pillage, spillage, tillage, village.

-illér, -illàr: chiller, driller, filler, griller, killer, miller, pillar, Schiller, spiller, swiller, thriller, tiller; distiller, Joe Miller, maxillar; caterpillar, killer-diller, ladykiller.

-illét: billet, fillet, millet, quillet, rillet, skillet, Willett.

-illiant: brilliant; resilient.

-illiàrds: billiards, milliards, mill-yards.

-illing: billing, shilling, willing; unwilling. (And extend -ill for "drilling", etc.)

-illiön, -illiàn: billion, Gillian, Lillian, million, pillon, trillion; carillon, Castilian, civilian, cotillion, pavilian, postilion, quadrillion, Quintilian, reptilian, vermilion; Marillian.

-illious: bilious, punctilious; antrabilious, supercilious.

-illōw: billow, kilo, pillow, willow; negrillo, armadillo, peccadillo.

-illy: billy, Billy, Chile, chili, chilly, filly, frilly, gillie, grilly, hilly, killi, lily, Lillie, Millie, Philly, Scilly, silly, shrilly, skilly, stilly, Tillie, Willie, Willy; Piccadilly, tiger lily, water lily, willy-nilly.

-ĭlöm: whilom, asylum.

-iltêr: filter, gilter, jilter, kilter, lilter, milter, philter, quilter, tilter, wilter.

-iltön: Chilton, Hilton, Milton, Stilton, Tilton.

-ily, -ighly: drily, Filey, highly, Reilly, Rilely, shyly, slily, smiley, wily, wryly.

-imáge: image; scrimmage.

-imáte: climate, primate; acclimate.

-imbêr: limber, timber, timbre; unlimber.

-imble, -ýmbàl: cymbal, fimble, gimbal, gimble (Lewis Carroll), nimble, symbol, thimble, tymbal, wimble.

-imbō: kimbo, limbo; akimbo.

-īmêr: chimer, climber, primer, rhymer, timer; begrimer, old-timer, sublimer.

-imic: chymic, mimic; alchimic, etymic; cherubimic, eponymic, metronymic, pantomimic, patronymic, synonymic.

-immy: gimmie, jimmy, Jimmy, shimmy.

-īmön, -ymàn: flyman, Hymen, limen, pieman, Simon, Timon, Wyman.

-impêr: crimper, limper, scrimper, shrimper, simper, whimper.

-imple: crimple, dimple, pimple, rimple, simple, wimple.

-imply: crimply, dimply, limply, pimply, simply.

-impy: crimpy, impi, impy, skimpy.

182

-imsy: flimsy, "mimsy" (Lewis Carroll), slimsy, whimsy.

-īmus: High Mass, primus, thymus, timous.

-īmy: blimey, grimy, limey, limy, rimy, slimy, stymie, thymy; "gorblimey".

-īna: china, China, Dinah, Heine, Ina, myna; regina; Carolina. (Compare -īnér.)

-īnàl: binal, crinal, final, rhinal, spinal, trinal, Vinal, vinyl; acclinal, caninal, declinal, equinal, piscinal; anticlinal, endocrinal, officinal, periclinal.

-incêrs: mincers, pincers, rinsers.

-inchêr: clincher, flincher, lyncher, pincher,

-incture: cincture, tincture, vincture.

-indêr: cinder, flinder, hinder, tinder; rescinder.

-indêr: Extend -ine for "blinder", etc.

-indle: brindle, dwindle, Hindle, kindle, spindle, swindle, windle, enkindle, rekindle,

-indnéss: blindness, kindness, color-blindness, loving-kindness.

-indy: Hindi, Lindy, shindy, windy.

-ineâr, -inniêr: finnier, linear, skinnier, whinnier.

-inely: finely; benignly, caninely, divinely, supinely; saturninely.

183

-inêr, -inör: diner, finer, liner, miner, minor, shiner, signer, winer, airliner, assigner, consignor, definer, designer, refiner.

-inĕt: ginnet, linnet, minute, spinet.

-inew, -inūe: sinew; continue, retinue; discontinue.

-inful: sinful, skinful. (Extend **-in.**)

-ingĕnt: stringent; astringent, constringent, contingent, restringent.

-ingêr: bringer, clinger, dinger, finger, flinger, linger, malinger, ringer, singer, slinger, springer, stinger, stringer, swinger, whinger, wringer, unslinger, unstringer.

-ingêr (soft "g"): ginger, injure. (And extend **-inge** for "cringer", etc.)

-ingle: cingle, cringle, dingle, ingle, jingle, mingle, shingle, single, springall, swingle, tingle, tringle; commingle, surcingle; intermingle.

-inglĕt: kinglet, ringlet, singlet.

-ingly: jingly, mingly, shingly, singly, tingly.

-ingō: bingo, dingo, gringo, jingo, lingo, stingo; Domingo, flamingo.

-ingy: cringy, dingy, fringy, stingy, twingy.

-ingy (with hard "g"): clingy, dinghy, springy, stringy, swingy.

-inic: clinic, cynic, finic, pinic, quinic, vinic;

aclinic, actinic, delphinic, fulminic, platinic, rabbinic; Jacobinic, monoclinic, narcotinic, nicotinic, polygynic.

-iniön, -inian: Binyon, minion, Ninian, pinion; Darwinian, dominion, opinion, Virginian; Carolinian, Carthaginian, Palestinian.

-inis: finis, Guinness.

-inish: finish, Finnish, thinnish, tinnish, diminish.

-īnish: brinish, nineish, swinish.

-inkêr: blinker, clinker, drinker, inker, shrinker, sinker, slinker, stinker, thinker, tinker, winker. (Extend -ink.)

-inkle: crinkle, inkle, sprinkle, tinkle, twinkle, winkle, wrinkle; besprinkle; periwinkle.

-inkling: inkling, sprinkling, tinkling, twinkling, wrinkling.

-inky: blinky, dinky, inky, kinky, pinky; Helsinki.

-inly: inly, thinly; McKinley.

-innêr: dinner, finner, grinner, inner, pinner, sinner, skinner, spinner, tinner, winner; beginner.

-innōw: minnow, winnow.

-inny: finny, guinea, Guinea, hinny, Minnie, ninny, pinny, Pliny, skinny, spinney, tinny, vinny, whinny, Winnie; Verginny, New

185

Guinea; ignominy.

-īnō: lino, rhino; albino.

-instêr: Leinster, minster, Minster, spinster; Westminster.

-intèl: lintel, pintle, quintal.

-intêr: dinter, hinter, minter, printer, splinter, sprinter, squinter, stinter, tinter, winter.

-intō: pinto, Shinto.

-intry: splintery, vintry, wintry.

-inty: Dinty, flinty, glinty, linty, minty, squinty; pepperminty.

-īnus: binous, dryness, highness, linous, Linus, minus, Pinus, sinus, spinous, vinous; echinus, salinous.

-īny: briny, liny, miny, piney, shiny, spiny, tiny, twiny, viny, whiney, winy; sunshiny.

-iön: Brian, ion, lion, Lyon, scion, Zion; anion, O'Brien, orion; dandelion.

-īpèd: biped, striped, typed, wiped.

-īpènd: ripened, stipend.

-īpêr, -ypêr: diaper, griper, piper, riper, sniper, striper, swiper, typer, wiper; bagpiper.

-īphön, -yphèn: siphon, hyphen.

-īpist, -īpèst: typist. (And extend -īpe.)

-ippêr: chipper, clipper, dipper, dripper,

flipper, gripper, kipper, nipper, ripper, shipper, sipper, skipper, slipper, snipper, stripper, tipper, tripper, whipper.

-ippét: sippet, skippet, snippet, tippet, whippet.

-ipple: cripple, nipple, ripple, stipple, tipple, triple.

-ippling, -ipling: crippling, Kipling, strippling, stippling, tippling.

-ippō: hippo, Lippo.

-ippy: chippy, dippy, drippy, grippy, hippy, lippy, nippy, snippy, zippy; Mississippi.

-ipstêr: tipster, whipster.

-ipsy: gipsy, "ipse", tipsy.

-iptic: cryptic, diptych, glyptic, styptic, triptych; ecliptic, eliptic; apocalyptic.

-iquant: piquant, secant; cosecant; intersecant.

-írà: Ira, Lyra, Myra, Thyra; Palmyra.

-īránt: gyrant, spirant, tyrant, virant; aspirant, conspirant, expirant.

-īrate: gyrate, irate.

-îrchén, -ûrchin: birchen, urchin.

-îrdâr, -îrdêr, -êrdêr, -ûrdêr: girder, herder, murder, sirdar; absurder, engirder, sheepherder. (Compare -îrter.)

-îrdle, -ûrdle: curdle, girdle, hurdle; engirdle.

(Compare -îrtle.)

-îrdlỹ: birdly, curdly, thirdly; absurdly.

-îreling: hireling, squireling.

-îrèn: Byron, siren, syren; environ.

-îrkin: See -êrkin.

-îrling, -êrling, -êarling, -ûrling: sterling, Stirling, yearling, whirling. (Extend -êarl.)

-îrlish, -ûrlish: churlish, girlish.

-îrloin: purloin, sirloin.

-îrmêr, -êrmêr, -ûrmûr: firmer, murmur, squirmer, termer; affirmer, confirmer, infirmer.

-îrmish: firmish, skirmish, squirmish, wormish.

-îrō: Cairo, giro, gyro, tyro; autogiro.

-irràh: mirror, sirrah.

-irrèl: Birrel, Cyril, squirrel, Tyrell, Tyrol, virile.

-irrup: chirrup, stirrup, syrup.

-îrtle, -ûrtle: fertile, hurtle, kirtle, myrtle, Myrtle, spirtle, turtle, whirtle. (See -îrdle.)

-îrty, -ûrty: Bertie, cherty, dirty, flirty, Gertie, shirty, skirty, spurty, squirty, thirty.

-īrus: Cyrus, virus; desirous, papyrus.

-īry, -īary, -īèry: briery, diary, fiery, friary, miry, priory, spiry, squiry, wiry; enquiry.

-isal: reprisal; paradisal.

-iscál: discal, fiscal.

-iscärd: discard, Liscard.

-iscount: discount, miscount.

-iscuit: See -iskét.

-iscus: discous, discus, viscous; hibiscus, lentiscus, meniscus.

-isect: bisect, trisect.

--isêr, -isōr: geyser, Kaiser, miser, sizar, visor; advisor, divisor, incisor; supervisor.

-ishêr, -issure: disher, fisher, fissure, swisher, wisher; kingfisher, well-wisher.

-ishŏp: bishop; fish-shop.

-isic: Chiswick, phthisic, physic; metaphysic.

-ision, -ission: scission, vision; abscission, allision, collision, concision, decision, derision, division, elision, envision, excision, misprision, precison, prevision, provision, recision, rescission, revision; circumcision, stratovision, subdivision, supervision, television. (See -ician.)

- isis: crisis, Isis, phthisis. (And compare plurals of -ice.)

-isit: visit; exquisite.

-isive: decisive, derisive, divisive, incisive; indecisive.

-iskêr: brisker, frisker, risker, whisker.

189

-iskĕt: biscuit, brisket, tisket, trisket, wisket.

-isky: frisky, risky, whisky.

-isly, izzly: Bisley, drizzly, frizzly, grisly, grizzly, sizzly.

-ismăl: dismal; abysmal, baptismal; cataclysmal, catechismal, paroxysmal.

-isŏn: See -izzen.

-īsŏn: bison, Meissen, Tyson.

-ispêr: crisper, lisper, whisper.

-issăl: See -istle.

-ission: See -ician.

-issūe: issue, fichu, tissue; atishoo, reissue.

-issure: See -ishêr.

-istănce: distance; assistance, consistence, desistance, existence, insistence, resistance, subsistence; co-existence, equidistance, inconsistence, inexistence, nonexistence, nonresistance. (Also -istant, -istĕnt + "s".)

-istănt: distant; assistant, consistent, existent, persistent, resistant, subsistent; coexistent, equidistant, inconsistent, inexistent, nonexistent, nonresistant, pre-existent.

-istĕn: christen, glisten, listen.

-istêr: bister, blister, glister, mister, sister, twister; assister, enlister, insister, persister, resister, subsister.

-isthmus: See **-istmás.**

-istic: cystic, fistic, mystic; **artistic, ballistic,** baptistic, Buddhistic, deistic, juristic, logistic, monistic, papistic, patristic, phlogistic, puristic, realistic, simplistic, sophistic, statistic, stylistic, theistic, touristic; agonistic, altruistic, animistic, annalistic, anarchistic, aphoristic, atheistic, cabalistic, canonistic, catechistic, Chauvinistic, communistic, dualistic, Eucharistic, eulogistic, euphemistic, euphuistic, familistic, fatalistic, humoristic, idealistic, intermistic, journalistic, Judaistic, methodistic, nihilistic, optimistic, pantheistic, pessimistic, polaristic, pugilistic, socialistic, syllogistic, talmudistic, unionistic; anachronistic, antagonistic, cameralistic, communalistic, dialogistic, formularistic, liberalistic, naturalistic, philosophistic, polytheistic, rationalistic, ritualistic, sensualistic; materialistic, spirtualistic; individualistic.

-istine (ēn): Christine, pristine, Sistine; Phillistine; amethystine.

-istle, -issál: bristle, fissile, gristle, istle, missal, missel, missile, scissel, sissile, thistle, whistle; abyssal, dismissal, epistle.

-istmás: Christmas, isthmus.

-istöl: Bristol, crystal, pistol.

-ītál: title, vital; entitle, recital, requital, sub-

191

title.

-ītêr: miter, niter. (And extend -ite and -ight.)

-īthêr: blither, either, lither, neither, tither, writher.

-ithêr: blither, dither, hither, slither, thither, whither, wither, zither.

-itian: titian. (See -ician. Compare -ision.)

-itic: critic; arthritic, mephitic, pleuritic, Semitic; aerolitic, analytic, biolytic, catalytic, diacritic, dialytic, eremitic, hypercritic, hypocritic, Jesuitic, paralytic, parasitic, stalactitic, tonsilitic, uranitic.

-ition: See -ician. (Compare -ision.)

-ītish: lightish, whitish. (Extend -īte.)

-itish, -ittish: British, fittish, kittish, skittish.

-itlêr: brittler, Hitler, littler, whittler.

-itnèss: fitness, witness.

-ittánce: pittance, quittance; acquittance, admittance, omittance, permittance, remittance, transmittance.

-ittèn: bitten, Britain, Briton, kitten, mitten, smitten, Witan, written; Thames Ditton.

-ittêr: bitter, "crittur", fitter, flitter, fritter, glitter, hitter, jitter, knitter, litter, pitter, quitter, sitter, slitter, spitter, splitter, titter, twitter; acquitter, committer, embitter, omitter, permitter, remitter, submitter, transmitter. (Compare -iddêr.)

-ittle, -ittâl, -ictual: brittle, knittle, little, quittal, skittle, spittle, tittle, victual, whittle, wittol; acquittal, belittle, committal, remittal, transmittal. (Compare -iddle.)

-itty: chitty, city, ditty, flitty, gritty, kitty, Kitty, nitty, pity, pretty, witty; banditti, committee.

-itûâl: ritual; habitual.

-ivâl: rival; archival, arrival, estival, outrival, revival, salival, survival; adjectival, conjunctival; nominatival.

-ivêl, -ivil: civil, drivel, rivel, shrivel, snivel, swivel; uncivil.

-ivên: driven, given, riven, scriven, shriven, shiver, sliver; deliver, forgiver.

-ivêt, -ivit: civet, pivot, divot, privet, rivet, shiver, sliver; deliver, forgiver; Guadalquivir.

-ivêr: diver, driver, fiver, hiver, Ivor, liver, shriver, skiver, sliver, stiver, striver, thriver; conniver, contriver, depriver, reviver, surviver.

-ivêt, -ivit: civet, pivot, divot, privet, rivet, trivet; Glenlivet.

-ivid: livid, vivid.

-ivöt: See -ivêt.

-ivy: civvy, dhivy, Livy, privy, skivvy, skivy, tivy; tantivy.

-ixêr, -ixîr: fixer, mixer; elixir.

-ixie: dixie, Dixie, nixie, pixy, tricksy, Trixie.

-ixture: fixture, mixture; admixture, commixture, immixture; intermixture.

-izård, -izzård, -issöred: bizard, blizzard, gizzard, izzard, lizard, scissored, vizard, wizard.

-izėn, -izzėn, -isön: dizen, mizzen, prison, wizen; arisen, bedizen, imprison.

-īzön: horizon. (False rhymes as "arisin' ".)

-izzier: busier, dizzier, fizzier, frizzier, vizier.

-izzêr: quizzer, scissor, whizzer.

-izzle: chisel, drizzle, fizzle, grizzle, mizzle, sizzle, swizzle.

-izzling: quisling. (And extend -izzle.)

-izzy, -usy: busy, dizzy, fizzy, frizzy, Lizzie, mizzy, tizzy.

-istic: cystic, fistic, mystic; deistic, fascistic, theistic; anarchistic, atheistic, bolshevistic, cabalistic, characteristic, communistic, pantheistic, polytheistic, socialistic, syllogistic, tritheistic.

-ōá: boa, Goa, moa, Noah, poa, proa; aloha, Genoa, Iowa, jerboa, Samoa; protozoa.

-ōadêr, -ōdör: goader, loader, odor; corroder, exploder, foreboder, malodor, unloader.

-ōafy: feofee, loafy, oafy, Sophie, strophe, trophy.

-ōakêr, -ōkêr, -ōchre: broker, choker, cloaker, croaker, joker, ocher, poker, smoker, soaker, stoker, stroker, yoker; convoker, provoker, revoker, uncloaker.

-ōakum, -ōcum: hocum, locum, oakum, Slocum.

-ōaly, -ōly, -ōley, -ōlly, -ōwly: coaly, drolly, goalie, holey, holy, lowly, molly, Rowley, shoaly, slowly, solely, wholly; roly-poly.

-ōamêr: comber, Cromer, foamer, Homer, omer, roamer; beachcomber, misnomer. (Compare -ōmà.)

-ōanêr, -ōnêr, -ōnör, -ōwnêr: boner, donor, droner, groaner, loaner, loner, moaner, Mona, owner, phoner, stoner; atoner, Corona, condoner, deponer, intoner, postponer; telephoner, Arizona. (Compare -ōnà.)

-ōapy: dopey, Hopi, mopey, ropey, soapy, topee.

-ôarish: boarish, whorish.

-ôarsêr: coarser, courser, forcer, hawser, hoarser.

-ôary, -ôry: dory, flory, glory, gory, hoary, lorry, more (Latin), storey, story, Tory; Old Glory, vain-glory; allegory, amatory, aratory, auditory, bibitory, category, cre-

matory, damnatory, desultory, dictatory,
dilatory,, dormitory, gradatory, **grallatory**
gustatory, hunky-dory, inventory, manda-
dory, migratory, monitory, negatory, offer-
tory, oratory, piscatory, predatory, prefa-
tory, probatory, punitory, purgatory,
repertory, rotatory, signatory, sudatory, territory, transitory, vibratory ; abjuratory,
adulatory, ambulatory, calculatory, circulatory, commendatory, compensatory, conciliatory, confirmatory, conservatory, declaratory, delineatory, depilatory, depository,
derogatory, dispensatory, exclamatory, explanatory, execratory, expiratory, incan-
tatory, incubatory, inspiratory, judicatory,
laboratory, liberatory, obligatory, observa-
tory, oscillatory, prohibitory, reformatory,
repository, respiratory, salutatory, speculatory, transpiratory, undulatory.

-ōastàl, -ōstàl: coastal, postal.

-ōastêr, -ōstêr: boaster, coaster, poster,
roaster, throwster, toaster; four-poster.

-ōatêr, -ōtêr, ōtôr: bloater, boater, doter,
floater, gloater, motor, noter, quoter, rotor,
scoter, toter, voter ; demoter, denoter, de-
voter, promoter; locomotor, rotomotor.

-ōaty: bloaty, coyote, Doty, Doughty, floaty,
goaty, throaty.

-obbêr: blobber, clobber, cobber, jobber, knob-

196

ber, lobber, robber, slobber, snobber, sobber, slobber, swabber, throbber; beslobber.

-obbin: bobbin, Dobbin, robbin, robin, Robin.

-obble: cobble, gobble, hobble, nobble, squabble, wobble.

-obby: bobby, Bobby, cobby, hobby, lobby, mobby, nobby, Robbie, snobby.

-ōbelēss, -ōblesse: noblesse, robelesse.

-ōbêr: prober, rober, sober; disrober, October.

-ōbōe: hobo, lobo, oboe, zobo; Launcelot Gobbo.

-obstêr: lobster, mobster.

-ōcàl: bocal, focal, local, phocal, vocal; yokel; bifocal.

-ōcean: See -ōtion.

-ōcêr, -ōsêr, ōssêr: closer, doser, grocer, grosser; engrosser, jocoser, moroser.

-ōchre: See -ōakêr.

-ockāde: blockade, brocade, cockade, dock-aid, okayed, stockade.

-ockêr: blocker, cocker, docker, knocker, locker, mocker, rocker, shocker, soccer, socker, stocker; knickerbocker.

-ockét: brocket, brockett, docket, locket, pocket, rocket, socket, sprocket; pickpocket, vest-pocket.

-ockney: cockney, knock-knee.

-ocky: cocky, crocky, flocky, hockey, jocky,

locky, rocky, Saki, stocky; sukiyaki.

-ōcōa, -ōcō, -ōkō: boko, coco, cocoa, loco, toko; baroco, rococo; Orinoco.

-oction: concoction, decoction.

-octŏr: doctor, proctor; concocter, decocter.

-ōcum: See -ōakum.

-ōcus: crocus, focus, hocus, locus, trochus; hocus-pocus.

-ōcust: focused, hocused, locust.

-ōdà: coda, Rhoda, soda; Baroda, pagoda, Fashoda.

-ōdàl: modal, nodal, yodel; trinodal; inter-nodal.

-oddèn: Flooden, hodden, sodden, trodden; downtrodden, untrodden.

-oddêr: codder, dodder, fodder, nodder, odder, plodder, prodder, solder. (Compare -otter.)

-oddèss, -odice: bodice, goddess.

-oddèst, -odèst: modest, oddest; immodest.

-oddle, -odèl: coddle, model, noddle, swaddle, toddle, twaddle, waddle; remodel. (Compare -ottle.)

-oddy, -ody: body, cloddy, Mahdi, noddy, shoddy, soddy, toddy, wadi; embody, nobody, somebody; anybody, busybody, everybody, Tom Noddy.

-odgêr: dodger, codger, lodger, stodger.

-odgy: podgy, splodgy, stodgy.

-odic: odic; anodic, exodic, iodic, melodic, methodic, parodic, rhapsodic, sarcodic, spasmodic, synodic; episodic, kinesodic, periodic.

-ōdium: odium, podium, sodium; allodium.

-odling: coddling, codling, godling, swaddling, toddling, twaddling, waddling; remodelling.

-odly: godly, oddly, twaddly; waddly; ungodly.

-ōdôr: See -ōadêr.

-ōdus: modus, nodus.

-ody: See -oddy. Compare -otty.

-ōĕm: poem, proem.

-ōey: blowy, Bowie, Chloe, doughy, goey, Joey, snowy, showy.

-ōfêr: chauffeur, gopher, loafer, Ophir, sofa.

-ôffēe: coffee, toffee.

-offêr: coffer, cougher, doffer, golfer, offer, proffer, scoffer.

-ôftên: coffin, often, soften.

-ofty: lofty, softy.

-ōgà: snoga, toga, yoga; Saratoga; Ticonderoga.

-ōgàn: brogan, Hogan, slogan.

-ōgey: bogey, bogie, fogey, stogie; Yogi.

-ôggish: doggish, froggish, hoggish.

-oggle: boggle, coggle, goggle, joggle, toggle;

199

boondoggle.

-oggy: boggy, cloggy, doggy, foggy, froggy, groggy, joggy, moggie, soggy.

-ōgle: bogle, fogle, ogle.

-ogrèss: ogress, progress.

-ōic: stoic ; azoic, heroic ; diapnoic, protozoic.

-oidêr: moider; avoider, embroider.

-oily: coyly, coily, doily, oily, roily. (Compare "loyally" and "royally".)

-oinêr: coiner, joiner; enjoiner, purloiner.

-ointmènt: ointment; anointment, appointment, disjointment; disappointment.

-oistêr, -oystêr: cloister, foister, hoister, moister, oyster, roister; Roister-Doister.

-oitêr: goiter, loiter, Ruyter; adroiter, exploiter; reconnoiter. (Compare -oidêr.)

-ōkay: bouquet, okay, Tokay, Touquet.

-ōkèn, -ōakèn: broken, oaken, token; bespoken, betoken, forespoken, foretoken, freespoken, outspoken, soft-spoken, unbroken, unspoken.

-ōkêr: See -ōakêr.

-ōkey: choky, cokey, croaky, hokey, joky, Loki, moky, oaky, poky, roky, smoky, yoky; okey-dokey, slow-pokey.

-ōlàr, -ōllêr, -ōwlêr: bowler, coaler, doler, droller, molar, polar, roller, solar, stroller, toller, troller; cajoler, comptroller, condoler, consoler, controller, enroller, extoller; patroller, unroller; circumpolar.

-ōldèn: golden, olden; beholden, embolden.

-ōldêr, -ōuldêr: bolder, boulder, colder, folder, holder, molder, older, polder, scolder, shoulder, smolder; beholder, enfolder, freeholder, householder, landholder, upholder.

-ōldly: boldly, coldly; manifoldly.

-ōleful: bowlful, doleful, soulful.

-olémn, -olumn: column, solemn.

-ōlèn, -ōlön: colon, Nolan, solen, solon, stolen, swollen; semi-colon.

-olic, -ollöck: colic, frolic, rollick; bucolic, carbolic, embolic, symbolic, systolic; alcoholic, apostolic, epistolic, metabolic, parabolic, vitriolic.

-olid, -ollied: dollied, jollied, dolid, squalid, stolid, volleyed.

-olish, -ollish: dollish, polish; abolish, demolish.

-ōlish: Polish. (Extend -ōle, -ōal.)

-ōlium: scholium; linoleum, petroleum.

-ollár, -olár, -olêr: choler, collar, dollar, dolor, loller, scholar, squalor, Waller.

-ollárd, -ollàred: bollard, collared, dollared,

Lollard, pollard, "scholard".

-ollége, -owlédge: college, knowledge; acknowledge, foreknowledge.

-ōllêr: See -ōlêr.

-ollét: collet, wallet.

-olliêr: collier, jollier.

-ollöp: collop, dollop, gollop, lollop, scallop, trollop, wallop.

-ollōw: follow, hollo, hollow, Rollo, swallow, wallow; Apollo.

-olly, -olley: Bali, collie, Dollie, dolly, Dolly, folly, golly, holly, jolly, Molly, polly, Solly, trolley, volley; finale, tamale; melancholy.

-ōlō: bolo, polo, solo.

--ōlon: See -ōlén.

-ölôred: colored, dullard.

-ölstêr: bolster, holster, oldster; upholster.

-ōltêr, -ōultêr: bolter, colter, jolter, molter, poulter; revolter.

-ōltish: coltish, doltish.

-olumn: See -olémn.

-ōly: See -ōaly.

-ōmà: coma, Roma, soma; aboma, aroma, diploma, Natoma, sarcoma, Tacoma; la paloma. (Compare -ōamêr.)

-ömách, -ummöck: hummock, stomach. (Add

202

"s" to rhyme with "flummox".)

-ōmāin: domain, ptomaine, romaine.

-ōmȧn, -ōwmȧn: bowman, foeman, gnomon, omen, Roman, showman, snow-man, yeoman; abdomen.

-ombat: combat, wombat.

-ombêr: bomber, omber, somber.

-ōmênt: foment (noun), loment, moment; bestowment.

-omêt, -omit: comet, vomit; Mahomet.

-omic: comic, gnomic; atomic; agronomic, anatomic, astronomic, autonomic, economic, gastronomic, metronomic, taxonomic.

-ōming, -umbing, -umming: coming, plumbing. (And extend **-um.**)

-ommȧ: comma, momma, rama; pajama.

-ommy: Tommy, mommy; bonhomie, salami.

-ōmō: chromo, Como, homo; major-domo.

ŏmpȧss: compass, rumpus; encompass.

-omptêr: compter, prompter; accompter.

-ōnȧ: Jonah, Mona; Arizona, Catriona, corona, Cremona, Iona, Verona; belladonna. (Compare **-ōanȇn, -ōwnêr.**)

-onȧge: nonage, Swanage.

-ondȧnt, -ondȇnt: fondant, frondent; despondent, respondent; correspondent.

-ondèl, -ondle: Blondel, fondle, rondle, Wandle.

-ondêr: blonder, bonder, condor, fonder, ponder, squander, wander, yonder; absconder, desponder, responder; corresponder.

-ōnely: lonely, only.

-ōnêr: See **-ōanêr.**

-onêst: connest, donnest, honest, wannest.

-öney: honey, money. (See **-unny.**)

-ôngêr: conger, longer, stronger, Tonga, wronger; prolonger.

-ônging: longing, thronging, wronging; belonging, prolonging.

-ôngly: longly, wrongly.

-ongō: bongo, Congo, pongo.

-onic: chronic, conic, phonic, sonic, tonic; adonic, agonic, bubonic, Byronic, canonic, carbonic, crotonic, cyclonic, demonic, draconic, euphonic, harmonic, hedonic, ionic, ironic, laconic, masonic, parsonic, platonic, sardonic, sermonic, Slavonic, symphonic, tectonic, Teutonic; Alcyonic, diaphonic, diatonic, embryonic, gramophonic, histrionic, macaronic, monophonic, philharmonic, polyphonic, telephonic, theogonic.

-öniön: See **-union.**

-onish, -onnish: donnish, wannish; admonish,

astonish, premonish.

-onky, -onkey: conkey, donkey; honky-tonky.

-önkey: As in "monkey"; see **-unkẏ.**

-ōnlẏ: lonely, only.

-önnàge, -unnàge: dunnage, Dunwich, tonnage.

-onnét: bonnet, sonnet.

-onny: Bonnie, bonny, Connie, Johnny, Lonny, Ronnie.

-onör, -onêr: goner, honor, wanner; dishonor.

-onsil, -onsul: consul, sponsal, tonsil; proconsul, responsal.

-öntàl: See **-untle.**

-ontract: contract, entr'acte.

-ōnus: bonus, onus, tonous.

-ōny, -ōney: bony, cony, coney, crony, drony, phony, pony, stony, tony, Tony; boloney, Marconi, polony, spumoni; alimony, antimony, macaroni, matrimony, parsimony, sanctimony, testimony.

-onẏx: onyx, phonics.

-ōōby: booby, looby, ruby, Ruby.

-ōōdle: boodle, doodle, feudal, noodle, poodle, strudel; caboodle, canoodle, flapdoodle; Yankee-Doodle. (Compare **-ōōtle.**)

-oody: goody, woody.

-ōōdy: broody, Judy, moody, Rudy.

-ookish: bookish, rookish, spookish.

-ooky: bookie, cookie, hookey, rookie.

-ōōky: fluky, spooky, Sukie.

-ōōlish, -ūlish: coolish, foolish, mulish.

-ōōnêr: See **-ūnår.**

-ōōnful: See **-ūneful.**

-ōōny, -ūny: loony, moony, pruny, puny, spoony, tuny. (And extend **-ōōn, -une.**)

-ōōpêr, -ūpêr, -ūpör: cooper, Cupar, drooper, duper, grouper, hooper, looper, scooper, snooper, stooper, stupor, super, swooper, trooper, whooper; recouper.

-ōōpy, -oūpy: croupy, droopy, loopy, rupee, soupy, whoopee, whoopy.

-ôorish: boorish, Moorish, poorish.

-ōōsêr: boozer, bruiser, chooser, cruiser, loser.

-ōōstêr: booster, rooster.

-ōōtêr: booter, chuter, cuter, fluter, hooter, looter, luter, mooter, muter, neuter, pewter, rooter, shooter, suitor, tooter, tutor; astuter, commuter, computer, disputer, freebooter, imputer, polluter, recruiter, refuter, saluter, uprooter; substitutor.

-ōōtle: brutal, futile, tootle; refutal. (Compare **-ōōdle.**)

-ōōty: beauty, booty, cootie, cutie, duty, fluty, fruity, rooty, snooty, sooty.

-ōōvêr: grover, prover; maneuver, Vancouver. (And extend -ōōve and -ove (ōōv) for "hoover", "remover", etc.)

-ōōzle, -oūsél, -ūsil: boozle, fusel, ousel; bamboozle, perusal, refusal.

-ōōzẏ: boozy, floosie, newsy, oozy, woosy.

-ōpàl: Bhopal, copal, opal; Constantinople.

-ōpêr, -ōapêr: coper, doper, groper, moper, roper, sloper, soaper, toper; eloper; interloper. (Extend -ōpe.)

-ophét: profit, prophet, Tophet.

-ophist: officed, sophist. (And extend -off for "doffest", etc.)

-opic: topic, tropic; myopic; horoscopic, microscopic, misanthropic, periscopic, stethoscopic, telescopic, theanthropic; heliotropic, kaleidoscopic, stereoscopic.

-ōpish: mopish, Popish.

-oplàr: poplar, toppler.

-oppêr: chopper, copper, cropper, dropper, hopper, lopper, mopper, plopper, popper, proper, propper, shopper, sopper, stopper, swapper, topper, whopper; grasshopper, improper, tiptopper; overtopper.

-opping: chopping, hopping. (Extend -op.)

-opple: hopple, popple, stopple, topple.

-oppy: choppy, copy, croppy, droppy, floppy, hoppy, loppy, moppy, poppy, shoppy, sloppy, soppy.

-opsy: copsy, dropsy, topsy, Topsy ; autopsy.

-optêr: copter; adopter; helicopter.

-optic: Coptic, optic; synoptic.

-option: option; adoption.

-ōpy, -ōapy: dopey, mopy, ropy, slopy, soapy, topee.

-ôrà: aura, Cora, Dora, flora, Flora, hora, Laura, mora, Norah, Torah; Andorra, angora, aurora, Endora, Pandora, signora; Floradora, Theodora. (And compare extensions of -ôre.)

-ôràge: borage, forage, porridge, storage.

-oràl: coral, laurel, moral, quarrel, sorrel ; Balmoral, immoral, unmoral.

-ôral: aural, choral, floral, horal, oral, thoral; binaural, femoral.

-örale: chorale, morale.

-ôran: Koran, Oran.

-ôrax: borax, corax, storax, thorax.

-ôrbèl: bauble, corbel, warble.

-ôrchàrd, -ôrchêr: orchard, tortured, Slorcha, scorcher, torture.

-ôrdêr, -ôardêr: boarder, border, corder, forder, hoarder, Lauder, order, warder; accorder, awarder, disorder, recorder, rewarder.

-ôrdial: curdial; primordial.

-ôrdön: Bordon, cordon, Gordon, Jordan, warden.

-ôrdship: lordship, wardship.

-ôrēäl, -ôriäl: voreal, oriel; armorial, memorial, pictorial; equatorial, immemorial; ambassadorial, conspiratorial, dictatorial, sinatorial; inquisitorial.

-orèign, -orin: florin, foreign, sporran, warren.

-ôrelock: forelock, Porlock, warlock.

-orènce: Florence, Lawrence, torrents; abhorrence. (Also **-àrrent** + "s".)

-ôrêr: borer, corer, floorer, gorer, porer, pourer, roarer, scorer, snorer, soarer, sorer, storer; adorer, deplorer, encorer, explorer, ignorer, implorer, restorer.

-ôrést, -ôrist: forest, florist, sorest.

-ôrgàn: gorgon, Morgan, organ; Glamorgan.

-ôrgêr: Borgia, forger, gorger, ordure; disgorger.

-ôrgi, -ôrgy: Corgi, Georgie, orgy.

-ôric: chloric, choric, doric, Warwick, Yorkrick; caloric, historic, phosphoric; allegoric,

209

categoric, metaphoric, paregoric, prehistoric, sophomoric.

-orid, -orrid: florid, forehead, horrid, torrid.

-oris: Boris, Doris, Horace, loris, Morris, Norris ; deoch-an-doras.

-ôrky: corky, door-key, porky. (Compare -ăwky.)

-ôrmâl: formal, normal; abnormal, informal.

-ôrmàn: doorman, floorman, foreman, Mormon, Norman, storeman; longshoreman.

-ôrmànt: dormant, torment; conformant, informant.

-ôrmêr: dormer, former, stormer, warmer; barn-stormer, conformer, deformer, informer, performer, reformer, transformer.

-ôrnêr: corner, Lorna, mourner, scorner, warner, yawner; adorner, suborner.

-ôrnèt: cornet, hornet.

-ôrning: horning, morning, scorning, adorning, suborning. (Extend -ôrn. Compare -ăwning.)

-ôrny: corny, horny, thorny.

-öröugh: borough, burro, burrow, furrow, thorough. (Compare -ûrrōw.)

-ôrus: chorus, Horus, porous, torous, torus; canorous, decorous, imporous, pylorus, sonorous; indecorous.

-ôrpör: torpor, warper.

-ôrpus: corpus, porpoise; habeas corpus.

-orrál, -orrél: See -orál.

-orrént: torrent, warrant; abhorrent.

-orrid: See -orid.

-orrör: horror; abhorror.

-orrōw: borrow, morrow, Morro, sorrow; tomorrow.

-orrý: Florrie, Laurie, lorry, quarry, soiree, sorry. (For rhymes to "worry", see -ûrry.)

-ôrsál, -ôrsél: dorsal, foresail, morsel; torsal.

-ôrsét: corset, Dorset.

-ôrtáge: cortege, portage.

-ôrtál, -ôrtle: chortle, mortal, portal, tortile; aortal, immortal.

-ôrtár, -ôrtêr: mortar, porter, quarter, shorter, snorter, sorter, sporter; assorter, consorter, contorter, distorter, escorter, exporter, importer, reporter, supporter, transporter. (Compare -ôrder.)

-ôrtèn: Horton, Morton, Norton, quartan, shorten, Wharton.

-ôrtex: cortex, vortex.

-ôrtion: portion, torsion, abortion, apportion, consortion, contortion, distortion, extortion, proportion. (Extend -ôrt for "contortion",

211

etc. Compare -ăution.)

-ôrtive: sportive, tortive; abortive, transportive.

-ôrtly, -ôurtly: courtly, portly.

-ôrtréss: court-dress, fortress, portress.

-ôrtune: fortune; importune, misfortune.

-ôrture: See -ôrchêr.

-ôrty: forty, porty, rorty, snorty, sortie, sporty, warty. (Compare -aughtý.)

-ôrum: forum, jorum, quorum, Shoreham; decorum; ad valorem, cockalorem, indecorum, pons asinorum.

-ôrus, -ăurus: aurous, chorus, chlorous, porous, taurus, torus; canorous, decorous, imporous, sonorous.

-ôrway: doorway, Norway.

-ôry: dory, flory, glory, gory, hoary, lory, oary, shory, snory, story, tory, whory; vainglory; allegory, a priori, auditory, category, crematory, dictatory, dormitory, gradatory, hunky-dory, laudatory, mandatory, migratory, monitory, narratory, piscatory, predatory, purgatory, sanitory, territory, transitory, vibratory; ambulatory, aspiratory, circulatory, conciliatory, conservatory, declaratory, depilatory, derogatory, exclamatory, expiratory, explanatory, gladiatory, inflammatory, judicatory, obligatory, osculatory, premonitory, preparatory, prohibitory, reformatory, repository, respiratory, retributory, revocatory, salutatory, speculatory, supplicatory, transpiratory, vindicatory; retaliatory.

-ōsely: closely; jocosely, morosely, verbosely.

-ōsà: Formosa, mimosa; amorosa.

-ōsèn: chosen, frozen, squozen; boatswain.

-osét, -osit: closet, posit, posset; deposit.

-oshêr: cosher, Kasher, posher, swasher, washer.

-ōsiêr: cosier, crozier, dozier, hosier, osier, mosier, rosier. (Extend -ōse. Compare -osure.)

-ōsion: corrosion, erosion, explosion. (Compare -ōtion.)

-ōsive: corrosive, erosive, explosive; inexplosive.

-osky: bosky, drosky.

-osmic: cosmic, osmic.

-ossacks: Cossacks, Trossachs.

-ôsságe: Osage, bossage, sausage.

-ôssêr, bosser, crosser, dosser, josser, prosser, tosser; emboser. (Extend -ôss.)

-ossum: blossom, possum; oppossum.

-ôssy: bossy, drossy, Flossie, flossy, glossy,

213

mossy, posse, tossy.

-ostàl, -ostèl: costal, hostel, hostile, postil; pentecostal.

-ōstàl: coastal, postal.

-ostêr: coster, foster, Gloucester, roster; accoster, imposter; paternoster, Pentecoster.

-ōstêr: See -ōastêr.

-ōstèss: ghostess, hostess.

-ostic: caustic, gnostic, joss-stick; accostic, acrostic, agnostic, prognostic; anacrostic, diagnostic, pentacostic.

-ostle, -ossil: docile, dossil, fossil, jostle, throstle, wassail; apostle, colossal.

-ostlêr: hostler, jostler, ostler, wassailer.

-ōstly: ghostly, mostly.

-ostrèl, -ostril: costrel, nostril.

-ostrum: nostrum, rostrum.

-ōsure: closure; composure, disclosure, enclosure, exposure, foreclosure. (Compare -osiêr.)

-ōsy, -ōzy: cozy, dozy, Josie, mosey, nosy, posy, prosy, Rosie, rosy.

-ōtà: quota, rota; Bogota, Dakota, iota, Minnesota. (Compare -ōater.)

-ōtàl: dotal, notal, rotal, total; teetotal; anecdotal, antidotal, extradotal, sacerdotal,

214

tcetotal.

-ōtàrd: dotard, motored.

-otchêr: blotcher, botcher, notcher, splotcher, watcher; top-notcher.

-ōtêr, -ōtör: See **-ōatêr.**

-othêr: bother, father, pother.

-öthêr: brother, mother, other, smother; another, Anstruther.

-ōthing: clothing, loathing.

-otic: azotic, chaotic, despotic, erotic, exotic, hypnotic, neurotic, narcotic, quixotic; idiotic, patriotic.

-ōtion, -ōceàn: lotion, motion, notion, ocean, potion; commotion, devotion, emotion, promotion, remotion; locomotion. (Compare **-ōsion.**)

-ōtive: motive, votive; emotive, promotive; locomotive.

-otly: hotly, motley, Otley, squatly.

-otnèss: hotness, squatness.

-ottàge: cottage, pottage, wattage.

-ottèn, -ottön: cotton, gotten, rotten; begotten, forgotten, misgotten.

-ottêr: blotter, clotter, cotter, dotter, jotter, knotter, ottar, otter, plotter, potter, rotter, spotter, squatter, totter, trotter, yachter; globe-trotter. (Compare **-oddêr.**)

-ottish: schottische, Scottish, sottish.

-ottle: bottle, dottel, glottal, mottle, pottle, throttle, tottle, twattle, wattle. (Compare **-oodle**.)

-ottō: blotto, grotto, lotto, motto, Otto, Watteau; ridoto, what ho!

-otty: blotty, clotty, dotty, knotty, Lottie, spotty, totty.

-ōtum, -ōtèm: pro tem, quotum, totem.

-öuble, ubble: bubble, double, rubble, stubble, trouble.

-öublèt: doublet, sub-let.

-ouchêr: coucher, Goucher, poucher, sloucher, voucher.

-oudêr: See **-owdêr**.

-oudly: loudly, proudly.

-oughboy: cowboy, ploughboy.

-ōughboy: doughboy, hautboy.

-oughen: roughen, toughen.

-ôughty: See **-ăughty**.

-ōuldêr: See **-ōldêr**.

-ōulticed: poulticed. (And extend **-ōlt**.)

-oundêr: bounder, flounder, founder, pounder, rounder, sounder; compounder, confounder, dumfounder, expounder, impounder, profounder, resounder, surrounder.

-oundly: roundly, soundly; profoundly, un-soundly.

-ounsèl: council, counsel, groundsel.

-ountain: fountain, mountain.

-ountèr: counter, mounter; accounter, dis-counter, encounter, recounter, remounter, surmounter; reencounter.

-ounty: bounty, county, "mounty".

-oūpèr: See -ōōpèr.

-ŏuple: See -upple.

-oūpẏ: See -ōōpẏ.

-oûràge: borage, courage; demurrage, dis-courage, encourage.

-oûrish: currish, flourish, nourish.

-ourly: dourly, hourly, sourly.

-oûrney, -êrny: Burney, Czerny, Ernie, ferny, journey, tourney; attorney.

-ousàl: housel, spousal, tousel; arousal, ca-rousal, espousal.

-ousêr: See -owsêr.

-ŏusin: See -ŏzĕn.

-ousy, -owsy: blowsy, drowsy, frowsy, lousy, mousy.

-outêr: clouter, doubter, flouter, jowter, pouter, router, scouter, shouter, spouter, sprouter, touter.

-oūthful: See -ūthful.

-outy, -oughty: doughty, droughty, flouty, gouty, grouty, pouty, snouty, sprouty.

-ōvà: nova; Casanova, Jehovah; Villanova. (Compare **-ōvèr.**)

-ovàl: approval, disproval, removal, reproval; disapproval.

-ovèl: grovel, hovel, novel.

-ŏvèl: hovel, Lovel, shovel.

-ovemènt: movement; approvement, improvement.

-ŏvèn: covin, oven, sloven.

-ōvèn: cloven, woven; interwoven.

-ŏvèr: cover, glover, lover, plover, shover; discover, recover, uncover.

-ōvèr: clover, Dover, drover, over, plover, rover, stover, trover; moreover, pushover; helf-seas-over. (Compare **-ōvà.**)

-ōvetāil: dovetail, love-tale.

-ōwàge: stowage, towage.

-owàrd: See **-owêred.**

-owdêr, -oudêr: chowder, crowder, louder, powder, prouder.

-owdy: cloudy, dowdy, howdy, rowdy; pandowdy.

-owèl: bowel, dowel, Powell, rowel, towel, trowel, vowel; avowal; disembowel. (Compare -owl.)

-ōwêr: blower, goer, grower, knower, lower,
mower, ower, rower, sewer, slower, sower,
thrower; bestower; overthrower.

-owêr: bower, cower, dower, flower, Giaour,
power, shower, tower; endower, overpower.
(Compare -our.)

-owêred: coward, Howard. (Extend -owêr,
-our.)

-owêry: bowery, cowry, dowry, flowery, houri,
showery, towery.

-ōwing: blowing, crowing, flowing, glowing,
going, growing, knowing, mowing, owing,
rowing, sewing, showing, snowing, sowing,
towing, throwing. (Extend -ōw + "ing".)

-owlédge: See -ollège.

-ōwlêr: See -ōlàr.

-ōwmàn: See -ōmàn.

-ōwnêr: See -ōanêr.

-ownsmàn: gownsman, roundsman, towns-
man.

-owny, -ownie: brownie, browny, downy,
frowny, Rowney, towny.

-owsêr: Browser, browser, dowser, grouser,
Mauser, mouser, rouser, towser, trouser;
carouser, espouser.

-ōwy: blowy, Bowie, Chloe, doughy, glowy,

goey, Joey, showy, snowy.

-oxèn: cockswain, oxen, Oxon.

-oxy: Coxey, doxy, foxy, poxy, proxy; Biloxi; orthodoxy, paradoxy; heterodoxy.

-oyal: loyal, royal; disloyal. (Compare **-oil.**)

-oyàlty: loyalty, royalty.

-oyànt: bouyant, clairvoyant, flamboyant.

-oyêr: annoyer, destroyer, employer, enjoyer.

-oyly: See **-oily.**

-oymènt: deployment, employment, enjoyment; unemployment.

-özèn, -öusin: cousin, cozen, dozen.

-özèn: See **-ösèn.**

-ozzle, -osel: losel, nozzle, sozzle, schnozzle; schlemmozzle.

-ūàl: See **-ūèl.**

-ūànt: fluent, truant; diluent, pursuant.

-uäve: suave, Zouave.

-ūbà: Cuba, tuba.

-ubbêr: blubber, clubber, drubber, dubber, grubber, lubber, rubber, scrubber, slubber, snubber, stubber, tubber; landlubber; india-rubber.

-ubbêred: blubbered, cupboard, Hubbard, rubbered.

-ubbish: cubbish, clubbish, grubbish, rubbish,

tubbish.

-ubble: See **-öuble.**

-ubbly bubbly, doubly, knubbly, rubbly, stubbly.

-ubby: chubby, cubby, grubby, hubby, nubby, scrubby, shrubby, stubby, tubby.

-ūbic: cubic, pubic; cherubic.

-ublish: bubblish, publish.

-ūby: See **-ōōby.**

-uccör: See **-uckêr.**

-ūcênt: lucent; abducent, adducent, recusant, reducent, traducent, translucent.

-ūcial: crucial; fiducial.

-ūcid: deuced, loosed, lucid, mucid; pellucid.

-uckêr: bucker, chucker, clucker, ducker, mucker, pucker, shucker, succor, sucker, trucker, tucker; seersucker.

-uckét: bucket, tucket; Nantucket.

-uckle: buckle, chuckle, huckle, knuckle, muckle, stuckle, suckle, truckle; unbuckle; honeysuckle.

-uckled: cuckold. (And extend **-uckle.**)

-ucklêr: buckler, chuckler, knuckler, truckler; swashbuckler.

-uckling: buckling, duckling, suckling.

-ucky: ducky, lucky, mucky, plucky; unlucky,

Kentucky.

-ūcre: euchre, fluker, lucre, puker; rebuker.

-uction, -uxion: fluxion, ruction, suction; abduction, adduction, affluxion, construction, deduction, defluxion, destruction, effluxion, induction, influxion, instruction, obduction, obstruction, production, reduction, seduction, traduction; introduction, misconstruction, reproduction, superstruction; overproduction, superinduction.

-uctive: adductive, conductive, constructive, deductive, destructive, inductive, instructive, obstructive, productive, reductive, seductive, traductive; introductive, reconstructive, reproductive, superstructive.

-uddêr: "brudder", dudder, flooder, mudder, rudder, scudder, shudder, udder. (Compare **-uttêr.**)

-udding: hooding, pudding, wooding.

-uddle: cuddle, fuddle, huddle, muddle, puddle, ruddle. (Compare **-uttle.**)

-uddlêr: cuddler, huddler, muddler.

-uddy: bloody, buddy, cruddy, muddy, ruddy, studdy, study. (Compare **-utty.**)

-ūdênt: prudent, student; concludent, imprudent; jurisprudent.

-ūdêr, -ūdôr: Tudor. (And extend **-ūde** for "ruder", etc.)

222

-udgeon: bludgeon, dudgeon, gudgeon; curmudgeon.

-ūdish: blue-dish, crudish, dudish, lewdish, nudish, prudish, rudish, shrewdish.

-ūdist: Buddhist, crudist, feudist, lewdest, nudest, nudist, rudest, shrewdest.

-ūdō: judo, pseudo; escudo.

-ūĕl: crewel, cruel, dual, duel, Ewell, fuel, gruel, jewel, newel; bejewel, eschewal, pursual, renewal. (Compare -ōōl and -ule.)

-ūĕnt: See -ūănt.

-ūĕt: chuet, cruet, Hewett, suet.

-ūĕy̆: See -ewy̆.

-uffêr: bluffer, buffer, cuffer, duffer, gruffer, huffer, luffer, puffer, rougher, snuffer, stuffer, suffer, tougher. (And extend -uff and -ough.)

-uffin: muffin, puffin; raggamuffin, roughen.

-uffing: bluffing, cuffing, huffing, puffing, roughing, ruffing, stuffing.

-uffle: buffle, duffel, muffle, ruffle, scuffle, shuffle, snuffle, truffle.

-uffling: muffling, ruffling, scuffling, shuffling, snuffling; unruffling.

-uffly: bluffly, gruffly, muffly, roughly, ruffly, scuffly, sluffly, toughly, truffly.

-uffy̆: bluffy, buffy, chuffy, fluffy, huffy,

pluffy, puffy, sloughy, snuffy, stuffy.

-ufty, -ufti: mufti, tuftly.

-ūgàl, -ūgle: bugle, frugal, fugal; McDougall; centrifugal.

-uggêr: bugger, drugger, hugger, lugger, mugger, plugger, rugger, shrugger, slugger, snugger, tugger; hugger-mugger.

-uggle: guggle, juggle, smuggle, snuggle, st.uggle.

-uggy: buggy, muggy, puggy, sluggy.

-ūgle: See **-ūgàl.**

-ugly: smugly, smuggly, snugly, ugly.

-ūicy: goosey, juicy, Lucy, sluicy; Debussy, retroussee.

-ūid: druid, fluid.

-uildêr: See **-ildêr.**

-ūin: bruin, ruin, Trewin.

-ūisánce: nuisance, usance.

-ūish: blueish, Jewish, newish, shrewish.

-ūitêr: See **-ōōtêr.**

-ūký: See **ōōky.**

-ūlá: Beulah, Eula, hula; Ashtabula, Boola-Boola, hula-hula. (Compare **-ōōlêr.**)

-ulgàr: Bulgar, vulgar.

-ulgénce: effulgenge, indulgence, refulgence; self-indulgence.

-ulgênt, fulgent; effulgent, emulgent, indulgent, refulgent; self-indulgent.

-ulky: bulky, hulky, sulky.

-ŭllah: mullah, nullah; Abdullah. (Compare **-ullêr.**)

-ullârd: dullard, colored.

-ullêr, -ŏlôr: color, cruller, culler, duller, guller, luller, sculler; annuller, discolor, medullar, tricolor; multicolor, technicolor, water color. (Compare **-ŭllah.**)

-ullêt (-ool): bullet, pullet.

-ullêt: cullet, gullet, mullet.

-ullion: cullion, mullion, scullion; rapscallion.

-ully (-ool): bully, fully, pulley, woolly. (And many false rhymes in adverbs ending in **-ully,** thus "beautifully", etc.)

-ully: cully, dully, gully, hully, sully, Tully.

-ulpit: bull-pit, pulpit.

-ulsion: pulsion; compulsion, convulsion, divulsion, emulsion, expulsion, impulsion, propulsion, repulsion, revulsion.

-ulsive: compulsive, convulsive, divulsive, emulsive, expulsive, impulsive, propulsive, repulsive, revulsive.

-ultry: sultry; adult'ry.

-ulture: culture, multure, vulture; agricul-

225

ture, horticulture, pisciculture, sylviculture, viticulture.

-ūlū: Lulu, pulu, Zulu; Honolulu.

-ūly, -ūely, -ewly, -ōōlie, -ōōly: bluely, coolie, coolly, cruelly, Dooley, duly, Julie, newly, ruly, truly, viewly; unduly, unruly, untruly.

-ūmà: Duma, puma, Yuma; Montezuma.

-ūmàge: fumage, plumage, roomage.

-ūmàn: cueman, Crewe-man, crewman, human, Kew-man, Krooman, lumen, Newman, pew-man, Truman; acumen, albumen, bitumen, legumen; superhuman.

-umbàr, -umbêr: cumber, Humber, lumbar, lumber, number, Rumba, slumber, umber; cucumber, encumber, outnumber; disencumber.

-umbêr: See **-ummêr**.

-umble: bumble, crumble, dumb-bell, fumble, grumble, humble, jumble, mumble, rumble, scumble, stumble, tumble, umble.

-umbly, -omely: comely, crumbly, dumbly, grumbly, humbly, numbly.

-umbril: tumbril, umbril.

-umbō: Dumbo, gumbo; mumbo-jumbo.

-ūmèn: See **-umàn**.

-ūmêr: See **-ūmŏr**.

-ūmid: fumid, humid, tumid.

226

-ummêr, -umbêr: comer, crumber, drummer, dumber, glummer, grummer, gummer, hummer, mummer, number, plumber, dummer, scummer, strummer, summer; midsummer.

-ummit: plummet, summit.

-ummy; chummy, crumby, crummy, drummy, dummy, gummy, lummy, mummy, plummy, rummy, scrummy, scummy, thrummy, tummy, yummy.

-umnàl: autumnal, columnal.

-ūmôr, -ūmêr, -ōōmêr: bloomer, boomer, doomer, fumer, humor, roomer, rumor, tumor; consumer, entomber; ill-humor, presumer.

-ūmous: fumous, glumous, grumous, humous, humus, plumous, spumous, strumous.

-umpêr: bumper, dumper, jumper, lumper, mumper, plumper, pumper, stumper.

-umpét: crumpet, strumpet, trumpet.

-umpish: bumpish, dumpish, grumpish, humpish, jumpish, lumpish, mumpish, plumpish, slumpish.

-umpkin: bumpkin, lumpkin, pumpkin.

-umple: crumple, rumple.

-umption: gumption, sumption; assumption, consumption, presumption, resumption.

-umptious: bumptious, gumptious, scrumptious; assumptious.

-umpus, -ömpàss: compass, rumpus; encompass.

-ūnà: luna, una; fortuna, lacuna, vicuna.

-ūnàr, -ūnêr, -ōōnêr: crooner, lunar, pruner, schooner, sooner, spooner, swooner, tuner; attuner, ballooner, communer, harpooner, lacunar, lampooner, sublunar, translunar.

-uncheön: luncheon, muncheon, puncheon, truncheon.

-uncle: Funchal, truncal, uncle; carbuncle, siphuncle.

-unction: function, junction, unction; compunction, conjunction, defunction, disjunction, expunction, injunction, subjunction.

-unctive: adjunctive, conjunctive, disjunctive, subjunctive.

-uncture: juncture, puncture; conjuncture, compuncture.

-undànce: abundance, redundance; superabundance.

-undànt; abundant, redundant; superabundant.

-unday: See **-undy.**

-undêr: blunder, dunder, plunder, sunder, thunder, wonder; asunder, fecunder, jocunder, refunder, rotunder, thereunder; thereinunder.

228

-undle: bundle, Blundell, rundle, trundle.

-undy, -unday: Grundy, Lundy, Monday, sundae, Sunday, undie.

-ūneful: spoonful, tuneful.

-ūnêr: See -ūnår.

-ungêr (soft "g"): blunger, lunger, plunger, sponger, spunger; expunger.

-ungêr (hard "g"): hunger, monger, younger; fishmonger, newsmonger; costermonger, ironmonger.

-ungle: bungle, jungle.

-ūnic: Munich, punic, runic, tunic.

-uniön: bunion, Bunyan, onion, ronion, Runyon, trunnion.

-unkård, unkêred: bunkered, drunkard.

-unkén: drunken, Duncan, shrunken, sunken.

-unkêr: bunker, drunker, dunker, flunker, junker, plunker, punker.

-unkét: junket, plunket.

-unkỳ: chunky, donkey, flunkey, funky, hunky, monkey, spunky, trunky.

-unlit: sunlit, unlit.

-unnåge: dunnage, gunnage, monage, tonnage.

-unnèl: funnel, gunwale, runnel, tunnel.

-unny, -öny, -oney: bunny, funny, gunny,

honey, money, sonny, sunny, tunny.

-unstêr: Dunster, funster, gunster, Munster, punster.

-untêr: blunter, bunter, grunter, hunter, punter, shunter, stunter; affronter, confronter.

-untle: frontal, gruntle; disgruntle, contrapuntal.

-upbōard: See **-ubbêred.**

-ūpid: Cupid, stupid.

-ūpil, ūple: pupil, scruple; octuple, quintuple, septuple, sextuple.

-uplèt: octuplet, quituplet, septuplet, sextuplet.

-ūplèt: drupelet ; quadruplet.

-uppêr: crupper, scupper, supper, upper.

-upple: couple, supple.

-uppý: guppy, puppy.

-ūrà: pleura, sura; bravura, caesura, datura; Angostura, Cuticura; coloratura; appoggiatura.

-ūràl: crural, jural, mural, neural, pleural, plural, rural, Ural; intermural, intramural, sinecural.

-ūrànce: durance; assurance, endurance, insurance; reassurance.

-ûrbàn: bourbon, Durban, turban, urban;

230

suburban.

-ûrbêr, -ûrbâr: curber, Durbar; disturber, per-
turber, superber.

-ûrbish: furbish, Serbish; refurbish, superbish.

-ûrchásed, -ûrchést: purchased. (And extend
-êarch, -êrch, -îrch, -ûrch for "birchest",
etc.)

-ûrdén: burden, guerdon, Purdon; disburden;
overburden.

-ûrdêr: See -îrdár.

-ûrdý, -îrdie: birdie, curdy, Ferdie, sturdy,
Verdi, wordy; hurdy-gurdy.

-ûreau: bureau, Douro, Truro, futuro.

-ûrelý: purely; demurely, maturely, obscure-
ly, securely.

-uremént: abjurement, allurement, conjure-
ment, immurement, obscurement, procure-
ment.

-ûrêr: curer, führer, juror, lurer, moorer,
poorer, purer, surer, tourer; abjurer, ad-
jurer, allurer, assurer, conjurer, demurer,
endurer, ensurer, maturer, procurer, se-
curer.

-ûrfý: Murphy, scurfy, surfy, turfy.

-ûrgent: purgent, surgent, turgent, urgent;
convergent, detergent, divergent, emergent,
insurgent, resurgent.

231

-ûrgeön: bourgeon, Sir John, Spurgeon, sturgeon, surgeon, virgin.

-ûrgẏ: See -êrgẏ.

-ûrist, -ûrést: jurist, poorest, purist, tourist; caricaturist. (And extend -ûre for "purest", etc.)

-ûrious: curious, furious, spurious; Asturias, incurious, injurious, juxurious, penurious, usurious.

-ûrky: See -êrky.

-ûrlêr: burler, curler, furler, hurler, pearler, purler, skirler, twirler, whirler.

-ûrlew: curlew, purlieu.

-ûrling: See -îrling.

-ûrlish: See -îrlish.

-ûrlẏ: See -earlẏ.

-ûrmá: Burma, derma, Irma, syrma.

-ûrmûr: See -îrmêr.

-ûrnêr: See -êarnêr.

-ûrnét: burnet, gurnet, ternate; alternate.

-ûrnish: burnish, furnish, sternish.

-ûrör: furor, juror. (And extend -ôor and -ure for "poorer", "surer", etc.)

-ûrriêr: currier, furrier, hurrier, skurrier, spurrier, worrier.

232

-ûrrōw: burrow, furrow. (Compare -örōugh.)

-ûrry̆: burry, curry, flurry, furry, hurry, Murray, scurry, slurry, Surrey, worry.

-ûrsàr, -ûrsêr: See -êrcêr.

-ûrtàin: See -êrtàin.

-ûrtle: See -îrtle.

-ûrvànt: See -êrvànt.

-ûrvey: purvey, survey.

-ûruy: See -êrvy.

-ūry, -ewry, ōōry: brewery, Drury, ewry, fury, houri, Jewry, jury, moory; Missouri.

-ūsà: Sousa, Susa; Medusa; Tuscaloosa.

-uscàn: dusken, Tuscan; Etruscan, molluscan.

-uscle, -ussél, -ustle: bustle, hustle, justle, muscle, mussel, Russell, rustle, tussle; corpuscle.

-ūsêr: See -ōōsêr.

-ushêr: blusher, brusher, crusher, flusher, gusher, husher, plusher, rusher, usher.

-ushy: brushy, cushy, gushy, lushy, mushy, plushy̆, rushy, slushy.

-ushy (-ooshy): Bushey, bushy, wushy, pushy,

-ūsion: fusion; allusion, collusion, conclusion, confusion, contusion, delusion, diffusion, effusion, elusion, exclusion, extrusion, illusion, inclusion, infusion, intrusion, Mal-

233

thusian, obtrusion, obtusion, occlusion, pertusion, profusion, protusion, reclusion, seclusion, suffusion, transfusion; circumfusion, disillusion. (Compare -ūtion.)

-ūsive: abusive, allusive, collusive, conclusive, conducive delusive, diffusive, effusive, exclusive, illusive, inclusive, infusive, intrusive, obtrusive, reclusive, seclusive; inconclusive.

-uskin: buskin, Ruskin.

-usky: dusky, husky, musky, tusky.

-ūsō: Crusoe, trousseau; Caruso.

-ussèt: gusset, russet.

-ussiá: Prussia, Russia.

-ussián: Prussian, Russian; concussion, discussion, percussion, repercussion.

-ussive: concussive, discussive, percussive; repercussive.

-ussy: fussy, Gussie, hussy, mussy.

-ustàrd: blustered, bustard, clustered, custard, flustered, mustard, mustered.

-ustêr: bluster, cluster, Custer, duster, fluster, juster, luster, lustre, muster, thruster, truster; adjuster, distruster, robuster; coadjuster, filibuster.

-ustful: lustful, trustful; disgustful, distrustful, mistrustful.

234

-ustian: fustian, combustion.

-ustic: fustic, rustic.

-ustice: custis, justice; Augustus.

-ûrvỳ: See -êrvỳ.

-ustle: See -uscle.

-ustlêr: bustler, hustler, rustler, tussler.

-ustly: justly; augustly, robustly, unjustly.

-ustöm: custom, frustum; accustom.

-usty: busty, dusty, gusty, lusty, musty, rusty, trusty.

-usy: busy, dizzy. (See -izzy.)

-ûtàl: See -ōōtle.

-ûthful: ruthful, toothful, truthful, youthful; untruthful.

-ûthlêss: ruthless, toothless, truthless.

-ûtile: futile, utile; inutile.

-ûtion: ablution, dilution, locution, pollution, solution, volution; absolution, allocution, attribution, collocution, condecution, constitution, contribution, convolution, distitution, devolution, diminution, dissolution, distrubution, elocution, evolution, execution, institution, envolution, Lilliputian, persecution, prosecution, prostitution, resolution, restitution, retribution, revolution, substitution; circumlocution, circumvolution, electrocution, interlocution, irresolution. (Compare

235

-ūsion.)

-ūtist: cutest, flutist, lutist, mutest, pharmaceutist, therapeutist. (Compare -ūdist.)

-ūtive: indutive; coadjutive, constitutive, persecutive, resolutive.

-utlêr: butler, cutler, scuttler, subtler, sutler,

-utney: chutney, Putney, gluttony, muttony.

-ütön: Luton, Newton, Teuton.

-uttêr: butter, clutter, cutter, flutter, gutter, mutter, putter, shutter, splutter, sputter, stutter, utter; abutter, Calcutta, rebutter. (Compare -uddêr.)

-utish: ruttish, sluttish.

-uttle: buttle, cuttle, scuttle, shuttle, subtle; rebuttal.

-uttöck: buttock, futtock, puttock.

-uttön: button, Dutton, glutton, mutton, Sutton; unbutton; bachelor button.

-utty: butty, nutty, puttee, putty, rutty, smutty, tutty. (Compare -uddy.)

-ūty: See -ōōty.

-ūture: future, moocher, puture. suture.

-ūvial: pluvial; alluvial.

-uxiön: See -uction.

-uyêr: See -ìar.

-uzzle: guzzle, muzzle, nuzzle, puzzle.

-**uzzlêr**: guzzler, muzzler, nuzzler, puzzler.

-**uzzy**: buzzy, fuzzy, huzzy, Fuzzy-Wuzzy.

-**yán**: See -**lön**.

-**ycle**: cycle, Michael; Lake Baikal.

-**ycle**: sickle, bicycle, tricycle. (See -**ickle**.)

-**yer**: See -**iêr**.

-**ylon**: nylon, pylon, trylon.

-**ỳmbál**: See -**imble**.

-**ỳmbol**: See -**imble**.

-**ymên**: hymen, flymen (stage), piemen, Simon.

-**ỳmic**: See -**imic**.

-**ỳnchêr**: See -**inchêr**.

-**ỳnic**: See -**inic**.

-**ỳntax**: syntax, tin-tacks.

-**ypist**: typist. (And extend **ipe**.)

-**ỳptic**: cryptic, diptych, glyptic, styptic, triptych; ecliptic, elliptic; apocalyptic.

-**ỳrāte**: gyrate, irate, lyrate; circumgyrate, dextrogyrate.

-**ỳric**: lyric; butyric, empiric, satiric, satyric; panegyric.

-**yrön**: See -**iren**.

-**yrtle**: See -**ûrtle**.

-**ỳsmál**: See -**ismal**.

-**ỳthàm**: lytham, rhythm, Withem.

-**ỳstic**: See -**istic**.

GLOSSARY OF POETIC TERMS

accent: stress indicated by a (´) mark placed above certain emphasized syllables in a line of verse.
Ex.: The night is white.

alexandrine: a verse consisting of six iambic feet.

alliteration: close repetition of a consonant sound at the beginning of a word.
Ex.: She sells sea shells by the seashore.

amphibrach: a metrical foot of three syllables consisting of the following pattern.
Ex.: I sprang to | the stirrup.

anacrusis: an additional unaccented syllable at the begining of a line.

analogy: likeness between two different things.
Ex.: T's with our judgment as our watches, none.

anapest: a metrical foot consisting of two unaccented syllables followed by one accented syllable.
Ex.: Oh, he flies | through the air.

anaphora: repeated use of a word or group of words throughout a verse.
Ex.: I gave her cakes and I gave her ale
I gave her Sack and Sherry.

antepenult: the third syllable from the end

of a word.

Ex.: an*te*penult.

anthology: collection of poetry.

apostrophe: An inanimate object is addressed directly as if it were actually a listening person.

assonance: the repeated sound of similar vowels in accented syllables.

Ex.: *Like a diamond in the sky*.

ballad: a verse consisting of three stanzas and a conclusion. It is usually written in iambic or anapestic tetrameter. The rhyme scheme is ab-ab-bc-bc bc-bc.

ballad stanza: a verse consisting of four lines in which the first and third lines are in iambic tetrameter and the second and fourth lines are in iambic trimeter. The rhyme scheme is abcb.

blank verse: unrhymed iambic pentameter verse which was the standard form of the Elizabethan time.

Ex.: Tomorrow, and tomorrow, and tomorrow,

Creeps in this petty pace from day to day.   "Macbeth"—Shakespeare.

Broadside Ballad: a poem written on a large sheet of paper and sung by the street singers in the sixteenth century.

cacophony: harsh sounds which are used in poetry for effect.
Ex.: a quick sharp scratch.

cadence: the pattern arrangements of rhythm in verse.

caesura: a pause usually in the middle of a line.
Ex.: A little learning | is a dangerous thing.

catalexis: omission of one or more final unstressed syllables.
Ex.: Irish poets learn your trade.

complaint: a Rennaissance lyrical poem in which the speaker moans for his absent or unresponsive lover.

consonance: the repeated use of the same consonant sounds before and after different vowels. Ex.: tip-top trip-trap.

couplet: two successive rhyming lines of poetry.

dactyl: poetic foot consisting of an accented syllable followed by two unaccented syllables.
Ex.: possible, wonderful.

didactic: poetry that teaches a moral lesson such as Pope's "Essay on Man".

dimeter: a line of poetry consisting of two feet.

doggerel: irregular rhyming lines that are

made regular by accenting normally unaccented syllables.

Elegy: personal poem of mourning.

envoy: a concluding stanza that is shorter than the ones it follows.

epic: a long narrative poem describing a hero and his brave deeds and following a set form.
Ex.: Beowulf.

epic simile: an elaborately written comparison.

epigram: a short witty poem or a short pithy statement.

fable: a short moral tale in verse having animals as its main characters.
Ex.: Uncle Remus Stories.

feminine ending: an extra unaccented syllable at the end of a verse.
Ex.: ev*er*.

foot: basic unit of measurement in poetry consisting of two or more syllables, one of which is accented.

heptameter: a line of verse consisting of seven feet.

heroic couplet: a rhyming couplet of iambic pentameter used in the heroic poems of the eighteenth century.

hexameter: a line of verse consisting of six

feet.

hyberbole: exaggeration or overstatement.

hypermeter: the additon of one or more unaccented syllables at the beginning and end of a line of poetry.

iamb: one unaccented syllable followed by one accented syllable. This pattern is the most common one used in verse.
Ex.: The world is still deceived with ornament.

incremental repetition: the repetition of a line or lines with some slight variation to further the rhyme.

internal rhyme: a rhyme that is located within a line.
Ex.: The night is white.

invocation: the addressing of a God whose help is sought.

lampoon: a personal attack in poetry.
Ex.: Pope's "The Rape of the Lock".

lyric: songlike poem expressing the writer's emotions.

macaronic verse: verse containing a mixture of languages.

masculine ending: a word ending with an accented syllable.
Ex.: remark, resound, confer.

meter: the pattern of accented and unaccented syllables in a line of poetry.

monometer: a line of poetry consisting of one foot.

octave: the first eight lines of an Italian sonnet.

octometer: a line of poetry consisting of eight feet.

ode: a long lyrical poem characterized by lofty feelings.

onomatopoeia: sound of a word that suggests its meaning. Ex.: buzz, hiss, clang, bang.

ottava rima: right-line stanza of iambic pentameter using ab ab ab c c as its rhyme pattern.

paradox: a statement that is usually self-contradictory.
Ex.: That I may rise and stand.

pastoral: any poem concerning the country.

pentameter: a line of poetry consisting of 5 feet.

personification: the transfering of human qualities to inanimate objects.
Ex.: Time's hand.

poetic license: liberty for an author to use figures of speech and archaic words and to change form.

Poet Laureate: chief poet of England who

243

writes all of the official poetry for the government.

pyrrhic foot: two unstressed syllables.

quatrain: four-line stanza.

refrain: a line or lines repeated during a poem.

rhyme: repetition of similar sounds at regular intervals.

rhyme royal: a seven-line stanza of iambic pentameter using ababbcc as its rhyme pattern.

rondeau: a French verse form which consists of 15 lines in 3 stanzas with only two rhymes used. The first line of the first stanza is used as a refrain in the second and third verse.

run-on verse: a line of poetry which continues into the next line without a grammatical break.

sapphics: classical verse form of four lines named after the Greek poetess, Sappho.

scansion: the study of a line to determine the meter used and number of feet in a line.

septet: a stanza of six lines.

sestet: last six lines of an Italian sonnet.

Shakespearian sonnet: fourteen lines of iambic pentameter having three quatrains and a concluding couplet using abab cdcd efef

gg as its rhyme pattern.

simile: the comparison of two or more objects using like or as.

    Ex.: She walks in beauty, like the night.
                          (Byron)

sonnet: a fourteen-line poem of iambic pentameter following a set rhyme scheme.

Spenserian stanza: a nine-line stanza named after its originator Edmund Spenser.

spondee: two stressed syllables used as a substitute for an iamb.

    Ex.: watch out.

stanza: a group of lines of poetry used as a division of poetry.

stress: accent.

tercet: a group of three lines that rhyme.

terza rima: a three-line stanza that is joined by rhyme to the next stanza.

    Ex.: aba bcb.

tetrameter: a line of poetry consisting of four feet.

trimeter: a line of poetry consisting of three feet.

triplet: a three-line stanza usually with one rhyme.

trochee: poetic foot consisting of a long syllable followed by a short one.

Ex.: legal, hateful.

Vers de société: playful lyrical verse that is sophisticated and deals with social customs.

verse: a. a single line of poetry. b. particular form of poetry such as blank verse. c. a stanza.

villanelle: short poem consisting of several tercets and a conclusion using only two rhymes throughout.